THE CHERRY ORCHARD

THE CHERRY ORCHARD

ANTON CHEKHOV

This edition published in 2019 by Arcturus Publishing Limited
26/27 Bickels Yard, 151–153 Bermondsey Street,
London SE1 3HA

Typesetting by Palimpsest Book Production Limited

Cover design: Peter Ridley
Cover illustration: Peter Gray

AD006591UK

Printed in the UK

Contents

Introduction

A great story or play does not always have to rely on imaginative worlds or heroes pitted against crafty villains. Anton Chekhov found artistic clarity in everyday triviality, the day-to-day events we often take for granted that reveal more about human life than any fantasy. Drifting between tragedy and comedy, stories like 'The Steppe' and plays like *The Cherry Orchard* depicted a uniqueness found only in human modesty.

Born on 29 January 1860 in Taganrog, Russia, Chekhov's father, Pavel, was a poor grocer while his mother, Yevgeniya, was an avid storyteller to him and his five siblings. Chekhov worked alongside his father and took his mother's stories to heart, but would always consider his childhood dreary due to the family's poverty. When their grocery failed in 1875 and they decided to move to Moscow, Chekhov stayed behind to finish his studies. With aspirations of becoming a doctor, he reconnected with his family in 1879 and enrolled in medical school. During his studies, Chekhov supported his family financially as a freelance writer.

Honing his craft throughout his twenties while still a physician, His first efforts were mainly short comic sketches. As he matured as a writer, he began to experiment with combining tragedy and comedy. After years of writing lowbrow stories for magazines, he achieved his great breakthrough in 1888 with 'The Steppe', published in the literary review *Severny vestnik* (Northern Herald). A story about a child's journey to the Ukraine with a strong focus on internal dialogue and character motivation, 'The Steppe' was the first of many that solidified his position as a leading realist writer, and it earned him the Pushkin Prize.

Certainly not a one-trick pony, Chekhov tried his luck as a playwright. Developing his craft even further, Chekhov wanted to emphasise reality by placing more importance on characters and their emotions than on complicated plots. This can be seen in 'Ivanov', a story of a young man's suicide that explores the depth of his mental illnesses.

His final play, *The Cherry Orchard* (1904), culminated in everything Chekhov had developed: value in the mundane, a mixture of tragedy and comedy, and the focus on the emotions of his characters. The aristocratic Russian landowner, Ranevskaya, distraught over her son's death, must save her family estate by auctioning their precious cherry orchard. But her attachment to her home leaves her useless, and she can only watch as her former serf, now a wealthy merchant, Lophakin, surpasses the aristocracy through his purchase of the home's symbol of beauty. Through such a simple story, Chekhov captured the essence of early 20th-century Russia, from the shifting cultural roles following the end of serfdom to the rise of the middle class.

Chekhov had suffered from tuberculosis since his youth, and the disease eventually took his life at the young age of 44 on 15 July 1904. Remaining both doctor and prolific writer until his death, Chekhov's dedication to everyday human interactions inspired many to search for the meaningful story in their own lives.

TRANSLATOR'S
INTRODUCTION

The last few years have seen a large and generally unsystematic mass of translations from the Russian flung at the heads and hearts of English readers. The ready acceptance of Chekhov has been one of the few successful features of this irresponsible output. He has been welcomed by British critics with something like affection. Bernard Shaw has several times remarked: 'Every time I see a play by Chekhov, I want to chuck all my own stuff into the fire.' Others, having no such valuable property to sacrifice on the altar of Chekhov, have not hesitated to place him side by side with Ibsen, and the other established institutions of the new theatre.

It is not the business of a translator to attempt to outdo all others in singing the praises of his raw material. This is a dangerous process and may well lead, as it led Mr. Calderon, to drawing the reader's attention to points of beauty not to be found in the original. A few bibliographical details are equally necessary, and permissible, and the elementary principles of Chekhov criticism will also be found useful.

The very existence of *The High Road* (1884), probably the earliest of its author's plays, will be unsuspected by English readers. During Chekhov's lifetime it was a sort of family legend, after his death it became a family mystery. A copy was finally discovered only last year in the Censor's office, yielded up, and published. It had been sent in 1885 under the nom-de-plume 'A. Chekhonte,' and it had failed to pass. The Censor of the time being had scrawled his opinion on the manuscript, 'a depressing and dirty piece, – cannot be licensed.' The name of the gentleman who held this view – Kaiser von Kugelgen – gives another reason for the educated Russian's low opinion of German-sounding institutions. Baron von Tuzenbach, the satisfactory person in *The Three*

Sisters, it will be noted, finds it as well, while he is trying to secure the favours of Irina, to declare that his German ancestry is fairly remote. This is by way of parenthesis. *The High Road*, found after thirty years, is a most interesting document to the lover of Chekhov. Every play he wrote in later years was either a one-act farce or a four-act drama.

In *The High Road* we see, in an embryonic form, the whole later method of the plays – the deliberate contrast between two strong characters (Bortsov and Merik in this case), the careful individualization of each person in a fairly large group by way of an introduction to the main theme, the concealment of the catastrophe, germ-wise, in the actual character of the characters, and the creation of a distinctive group-atmosphere. It need scarcely be stated that *The High Road* is not a 'dirty' piece according to Russian or to German standards; Chekhov was incapable of writing a dirty play or story. For the rest, this piece differs from the others in its presentation, not of Chekhov's favourite middle-classes, but of the moujik [serf], nourishing, in a particularly stuffy atmosphere, an intense mysticism and an equally intense thirst for vodka.

The Proposal (1889) and *The Bear* (1890) may be taken as good examples of the sort of humour admired by the average Russian. The latter play, in another translation, was put on as a curtain-raiser to a cinematograph entertainment at a London theatre in 1914, and had quite a pleasant reception from a thoroughly Philistine audience. The humour is very nearly of the variety most popular over here, the psychology is a shade subtler. The Russian novelist or dramatist takes to psychology as some of his fellow-countrymen take to drink; in doing this he achieves fame by showing us what we already know, and at the same time he kills his own creative power. Chekhov just escaped the tragedy of suicide by introspection, and was only enabled to do this by the possession of a sense of humour. That is why we should not regard *The Bear*, *The Wedding*, or *The Anniversary* as the work of a merely humorous young man, but as the saving graces which made perfect *The Cherry Orchard*.

The Three Sisters (1901) is said to act better than any other of Chekhov's plays, and should surprise an English audience exceedingly. It and *The Cherry Orchard* are the tragedies of doing nothing. The three sisters have only one desire in the world, to go to Moscow and live there. There is no reason on earth, economic, sentimental, or other, why they should not pack their bags and take the next train to Moscow. But they will not do it. They cannot do it. And we know perfectly well that if they were transplanted thither miraculously, they would be extremely unhappy as soon as ever the excitement of the miracle had worn off. In the other play Mme. Ranevsky can be saved from ruin if she will only consent to a perfectly simple step – the sale of an estate. She cannot do this, is ruined, and thrown out into the unsympathetic world. Chekhov is the dramatist, not of action, but of inaction. The tragedy of inaction is as overwhelming, when we understand it, as the tragedy of an Othello, or a Lear, crushed by the wickedness of others. The former is being enacted daily, but we do not stage it, we do not know how. But who shall deny that the base of almost all human unhappiness is just this inaction, manifesting itself in slovenliness of thought and execution, education, and ideal?

The Russian, painfully conscious of his own weakness, has accepted this point of view, and regards *The Cherry*

Orchard as its master-study in dramatic form. They speak of the palpitating hush which fell upon the audience of the Moscow Art Theatre after the first fall of the curtain at the first performance – a hush so intense as to make Chekhov's friends undergo the initial emotions of assisting at a vast theatrical failure. But the silence was almost a sob, to be followed, when overcome, by an epic applause. And, a few months later, Chekhov died.

Lastly, the scheme of transliteration employed has been that, generally speaking, recommended by the Liverpool School of Russian Studies. This is distinctly the best of those in the field, but as it would compel one, *e.g.*, to write a popular female name, 'Marya,' I have not treated it with absolute respect.

Julius West, 1916

Characters

LUBOV ANDREYEVNA RANEVSKY (Mme. RANEVSKY),
a landowner

ANYA, *her daughter, aged seventeen*

VARYA (BARBARA), *her adopted daughter, aged
twenty-seven*

LEONID ANDREYEVITCH GAEV, *Mme. Ranevsky's
brother*

ERMOLAI ALEXEYVITCH LOPAKHIN, *a merchant*

PETER SERGEYEVITCH TROFIMOV, *a student*

BORIS BORISOVITCH SIMEONOV-PISCHIN,
a landowner

CHARLOTTA IVANOVNA, *a governess*

SIMEON PANTELEYEVITCH EPIKHODOV, *a clerk*

DUNYASHA (AVDOTYA FEDOROVNA), *a maidservant*

FIERS, *an old footman, aged eighty-seven*

YASHA, *a young footman*

A Tramp

A Station-master

Post Office Clerk

Guests

A Servant

The action takes place on Mme. Ranevsky's *estate*

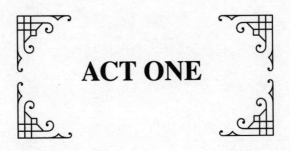

ACT ONE

[*A room which is still called the nursery. One of the doors leads into* ANYA'S *room. It is close on sunrise. It is May. The cherry-trees are in flower but it is chilly in the garden. There is an early frost. The windows of the room are shut.* DUNYASHA *comes in with a candle, and* LOPAKHIN *with a book in his hand.*]

LOPAKHIN. The train's arrived, thank God. What's the time?

DUNYASHA. It will soon be two. [*Blows out candle.*] It is light already.

LOPAKHIN. How much was the train late? Two hours at least. [*Yawns and stretches himself.*] I have made a rotten mess of it! I came here on purpose to meet them at the station, and then overslept myself... in my chair. It's a pity. I wish you'd wakened me.

DUNYASHA. I thought you'd gone away. [*Listening.*] I think I hear them coming.

LOPAKHIN. [*Listens.*] No.... They've got to collect their luggage and so on.... [*Pause.*] Lubov Andreyevna has been living abroad for five years; I don't know what she'll be like now.... She's a good sort—an easy, simple person. I remember when I was a boy of fifteen, my father, who is dead—he used to keep a shop in the village here—hit me on the face with his fist, and my nose bled.... We had gone into the yard together for something or other, and he was a little drunk. Lubov Andreyevna, as I remember her now, was still young, and very thin, and she took me to the washstand here in this very room, the nursery. She said, 'Don't cry, little man, it'll be all right in time for your wedding.' [*Pause.*] 'Little man'.... My father was a peasant, it's true, but here I am in a white waistcoat and yellow shoes... a pearl out of an oyster. I'm rich now, with lots of money, but just think about it and examine me, and you'll find I'm still a peasant down to the marrow of my bones. [*Turns over the pages of his book.*] Here I've been reading this book, but I understood nothing. I read and fell asleep. [*Pause.*]

DUNYASHA. The dogs didn't sleep all night; they know that they're coming.

LOPAKHIN. What's up with you, Dunyasha...?

DUNYASHA. My hands are shaking. I shall faint.

LOPAKHIN. You're too sensitive, Dunyasha. You dress just like a lady, and you do your hair like one too. You oughtn't. You should know your place.

EPIKHODOV. [*Enters with a bouquet. He wears a short jacket and brilliantly polished boots which squeak audibly. He drops the bouquet as he enters, then picks it up.*] The gardener sent these; says they're to go into the dining-room. [*Gives the bouquet to* DUNYASHA.]

LOPAKHIN. And you'll bring me some kvass.

DUNYASHA. Very well. [*Exit.*]

EPIKHODOV. There's a frost this morning—three degrees, and

the cherry-trees are all in flower. I can't approve of our climate. [*Sighs.*] I can't. Our climate is indisposed to favour us even this once. And, Ermolai Alexeyevitch, allow me to say to you, in addition, that I bought myself some boots two days ago, and I beg to assure you that they squeak in a perfectly unbearable manner. What shall I put on them?

LOPAKHIN. Go away. You bore me.

EPIKHODOV. Some misfortune happens to me every day. But I don't complain; I'm used to it, and I can smile. [DUNYASHA *comes in and brings* LOPAKHIN *some kvass.*] I shall go. [*Knocks over a chair.*] There.... [*triumphantly*] There, you see, if I may use the word, what circumstances I am in, so to speak. It is even simply marvellous. [*Exit.*]

DUNYASHA. I may confess to you, Ermolai Alexeyevitch, that Epikhodov has proposed to me.

LOPAKHIN. Ah!

DUNYASHA. I don't know what to do about it. He's a nice young man, but every now and again, when he begins talking, you can't understand a word he's saying. I think I like him. He's madly in love with me. He's an unlucky man; every day something happens. We tease him about it. They call him 'Two-and-twenty troubles.'

LOPAKHIN. [*Listens.*] There they come, I think.

DUNYASHA. They're coming! What's the matter with me? I'm cold all over.

LOPAKHIN. There they are, right enough. Let's go and meet them. Will she know me? We haven't seen each other for five years.

DUNYASHA. [*excited*] I shall faint in a minute.... Oh, I'm fainting!

[*Two carriages are heard driving up to the house.* LOPAKHIN *and* DUNYASHA *quickly go out. The stage is empty. A noise begins in the next room.* FIERS, *leaning on a stick, walks quickly across the stage; he has just been to meet* LUBOV ANDREYEVNA. *He wears an old-fashioned livery and a tall hat. He is saying something to himself, but not a word of it can be made out. The noise behind the stage gets louder and louder. A voice is heard: 'Let's go in there.' Enter* LUBOV ANDREYEVNA, ANYA, *and* CHARLOTTA IVANOVNA *with a little dog on a chain, and all dressed in travelling clothes,* VARYA *in a long coat and with a kerchief on her head.* GAEV, SIMEONOV-PISCHIN, LOPAKHIN, DUNYASHA *with a parcel and an umbrella, and a servant with luggage—all cross the room.*]

ANYA. Let's come through here. Do you remember what this room is, mother?

LUBOV. [*joyfully, through her tears*] The nursery!

VARYA. How cold it is! My hands are quite numb. [*To* LUBOV ANDREYEVNA:] Your rooms, the white one and the violet one, are just as they used to be, mother.

LUBOV. My dear nursery, oh, you beautiful room.... I used to sleep here when I was a baby. [*Weeps.*] And here I am like a little girl again. [*Kisses her brother,* VARYA, *then her brother again.*] And Varya is just as she used to be, just like a nun. And I knew Dunyasha. [*Kisses her.*]

GAEV. The train was two hours late. There now; how's that for punctuality?

CHARLOTTA. [*To* PISCHIN:] My dog eats nuts too.

PISCHIN. [*astonished*] To think of that, now!

[*All go out except* ANYA *and* DUNYASHA.]

DUNYASHA. We did have to wait for you!

[*Takes off* ANYA's *cloak and hat.*]

ANYA. I didn't get any sleep for four nights on the journey.... I'm awfully cold.

DUNYASHA. You went away during Lent, when it was snowing and frosty, but now? Darling! [*Laughs and kisses her.*] We did have to wait for you, my joy, my pet.... I must tell you at once, I can't bear to wait a minute.

ANYA. [*tired*] Something else now...?

DUNYASHA. The clerk, Epikhodov, proposed to me after Easter.

ANYA. Always the same.... [*Puts her hair straight.*] I've lost all my hairpins.... [*She is very tired, and even staggers as she walks.*]

DUNYASHA. I don't know what to think about it. He loves me, he loves me so much!

ANYA. [*Looks into her room; in a gentle voice:*] My room, my windows, as if I'd never gone away. I'm at home! To-morrow morning I'll get up and have a run in the garden....Oh, if I could only get to sleep! I didn't sleep the whole journey, I was so bothered.

DUNYASHA. Peter Sergeyevitch came two days ago.

ANYA. [*joyfully*] Peter!

DUNYASHA. He sleeps in the bath-house, he lives there. He said he was afraid he'd be in the way. [*Looks at her pocket-watch.*] I ought to wake him, but Barbara Mihailovna told me not to. 'Don't wake him,' she said.

[*Enter* VARYA, *a bunch of keys on her belt.*]

VARYA. Dunyasha, some coffee, quick. Mother wants some.

DUNYASHA. This minute. [*Exit.*]

VARYA. Well, you've come, glory be to God. Home again. [*Caressing her.*] My darling is back again! My pretty one is back again!

ANYA. I did have an awful time, I tell you.

VARYA. I can just imagine it!

ANYA. I went away in Holy Week; it was very cold then. Charlotta talked the whole way and would go on performing her tricks. Why did you tie Charlotta on to me?

VARYA. You couldn't go alone, darling, at seventeen!

ANYA. We went to Paris; it's cold there and snowing. I talk French perfectly horribly. My mother lives on the fifth floor. I go to her, and find her there with various Frenchmen, women, an old abbé with a book, and everything in tobacco smoke and with no comfort at all. I suddenly became very sorry for mother—so sorry that I took her head in my arms and hugged her and wouldn't let her go. Then mother started hugging me and crying....

VARYA. [*Weeping.*] Don't say any more, don't say any more....

ANYA. She's already sold her villa near Mentone; she's nothing left, nothing. And I haven't a copeck[1] left either; we only just managed to get here. And mother won't understand! We had dinner at a station; she asked for all the expensive things, and tipped the waiters one rouble each. And Charlotta too. Yasha wants his share too—it's too bad. Mother's got a footman now, Yasha; we've brought him here.

VARYA. I saw the wretch.

....
1   One rouble is worth 100 copecks.

ANYA. How's business? Has the interest been paid?

VARYA. Not much chance of that.

ANYA. Oh God, oh God...

VARYA. The place will be sold in August.

ANYA. O God....

LOPAKHIN. [*Looks in at the door and moos.*] Moo!... [*Exit.*]

VARYA. [*through her tears*] I'd like to.... [*Shakes her fist.*]

ANYA. [*Embraces* VARYA, *softly.*] Varya, has he proposed to you? [VARYA *shakes head.*] But he loves you.... Why don't you make up your minds? Why do you keep on waiting?

VARYA. I think that it will all come to nothing. He's a busy man. I'm not his affair... he pays no attention to me. Bless the man, I don't want to see him.... But everybody talks about our marriage, everybody congratulates me, and there's nothing in it at all, it's all like a dream. [*in another tone*] You've got a brooch like a bee.

ANYA. [*sadly*] Mother bought it. [*Goes into her room, and talks lightly, like a child.*] In Paris I went up in a balloon!

VARYA. My darling's come back, my pretty one's come back! [DUNYASHA *has already returned with the coffee-pot and is making the coffee,* VARYA *stands near the door.*] I go about all day, looking after the house, and I think all the time, if only

26

you could marry a rich man, then I'd be happy and would go away somewhere by myself, then to Kiev... to Moscow, and so on, from one holy place to another. I'd tramp and tramp. That would be splendid!

ANYA. The birds are singing in the garden. What time is it now?

VARYA. It must be getting on for three. Time you went to sleep, darling. [*Goes into* ANYA'S *room.*] Splendid!

[*Enter* YASHA *with a plaid shawl and a travelling bag.*]

YASHA. [*Crossing the stage; politely:*] May I go this way?

DUNYASHA. I hardly knew you, Yasha. You have changed abroad.

YASHA. Hm... and who are you?

DUNYASHA. When you went away I was only so high. [*Showing with her hand.*] I'm Dunyasha, the daughter of Theodore Kozoyedov. You don't remember!

YASHA. Oh, you little cucumber!

[*Looks round and embraces her. She screams and drops a saucer.* YASHA *goes out quickly.*]

VARYA. [*In the doorway; in an angry voice:*] What's that?

DUNYASHA. [*through her tears*] I've broken a saucer.

VARYA. It may bring luck.

ANYA. [*Coming out of her room.*] We must tell mother that Peter's here.

VARYA. I told them not to wake him.

ANYA. [*thoughtfully*] Father died six years ago, and a month later my brother Grisha was drowned in the river—such a dear little boy of seven! Mother couldn't bear it; she went away, away, without looking round.... [*Shudders.*] How I understand her; if only she knew! [*Pause.*] And Peter Trofimov was Grisha's tutor, he might tell her....

[*Enter* FIERS *in a short jacket and white waistcoat.*]

FIERS. [*Goes to the coffee-pot, nervously.*] The mistress is going to have some food here.... [*Puts on white gloves.*] Is the coffee ready? [*To* DUNYASHA, *severely:*] You! Where's the cream?

DUNYASHA. Oh, dear me...! [*Rapid exit.*]

FIERS. [*Fussing round the coffee-pot.*] Oh, you bungler.... [*Murmurs to himself.*] Back from Paris... the master went to Paris once... in a carriage.... [*Laughs.*]

VARYA. What are you talking about, Fiers?

FIERS. I beg your pardon? [*joyfully*] The mistress is home again. I've lived to see her! Don't care if I die now.... [*Weeps with joy.*]

[*Enter* LUBOV ANDREYEVNA, GAEV, LOPAKHIN, *and* SIMEONOV-PISCHIN, *the latter in a long jacket of thin cloth and loose trousers.* GAEV, *coming in, moves his arms and body about as if he is playing billiards.*]

LUBOV. Let me remember now. Red into the corner! Twice into the centre!

GAEV. Right into the pocket! Once upon a time you and I used both to sleep in this room, and now I'm fifty-one; it does seem strange.

LOPAKHIN. Yes, time does go.

GAEV. Who does?

LOPAKHIN. I said that time does go.

GAEV. It smells of patchouli here.

ANYA. I'm going to bed. Good-night, mother. [*Kisses her.*]

LUBOV. My lovely little one. [*Kisses her hand.*] Glad to be at home? I can't get over it.

ANYA. Good-night, uncle.

GAEV. [*Kisses her face and hands.*] God be with you. How you do resemble your mother! [*To his sister:*] You were just like her at her age, Luba.

[ANYA *gives her hand to* LOPAKHIN *and* PISCHIN *and goes out, shutting the door behind her.*]

LUBOV. She's awfully tired.

PISCHIN. It's a very long journey.

VARYA. [*To* LOPAKHIN *and* PISCHIN:] Well, sirs, it's getting on for three, quite time you went.

LUBOV. [*Laughs.*] You're just the same as ever, Varya. [*Draws her close and kisses her.*] I'll have some coffee now, then we'll all go. [FIERS *lays a cushion under her feet.*] Thank you, dear. I'm used to coffee. I drink it day and night. Thank you, dear old man. [*Kisses* FIERS.]

VARYA. I'll go and see if they've brought in all the luggage. [*Exit.*]

LUBOV. Is it really I who am sitting here? [*Laughs.*] I want to jump about and wave my arms. [*Covers her face with her hands.*] But suppose I'm dreaming! God knows I love my own country, I love it deeply; I couldn't look out of the railway carriage, I cried so much. [*through her tears*] Still, I must have my coffee. Thank you, Fiers. Thank you, dear old man. I'm so glad you're still with us.

FIERS. The day before yesterday.

GAEV. He doesn't hear well.

LOPAKHIN. I've got to go off to Kharkov by the five o'clock train. I'm awfully sorry! I should like to have a look at you, to gossip a little. You're as fine-looking as ever.

PISCHIN. [*Breathes heavily.*] Even finer-looking... dressed in
Paris fashions... confound it all.

LOPAKHIN. Your brother, Leonid Andreyevitch, says I'm a
snob, a usurer, but that is absolutely nothing to me. Let him
talk. Only I do wish you would believe in me as you once
did, that your wonderful, touching eyes would look at me as
they did before. Merciful God! My father was the serf of
your grandfather and your own father, but you—you more
than anybody else—did so much for me once upon a time
that I've forgotten everything and love you as if you
belonged to my family... and even more.

LUBOV. I can't sit still, I'm not in a state to do it. [*Jumps up
and walks about in great excitement.*] I'll never survive this
happiness.... You can laugh at me; I'm a silly woman.... My
dear little cupboard. [*Kisses cupboard.*] My little table.

GAEV. Nurse has died in your absence.

LUBOV. [*Sits and drinks coffee.*] Yes, bless her soul. I heard
by letter.

GAEV. And Anastasius has died too. Peter Kosoy has left me
and now lives in town with the Commissioner of Police.
[*Takes a box of sugar-candy out of his pocket and sucks a
piece.*]

PISCHIN. My daughter, Dashenka, sends her love.

LOPAKHIN. I want to say something very pleasant, very delightful, to you. [*Looks at his watch.*] I'm going away at once, I haven't much time... but I'll tell you all about it in two or three words. As you already know, your cherry orchard is to be sold to pay your debts, and the sale is fixed for August 22; but you needn't be alarmed, dear madam, you may sleep in peace; there's a way out. Here's my plan. Please attend carefully! Your estate is only thirteen miles from the town, the railway runs by, and if the cherry orchard and the land by the river are broken up into building lots and are then leased off for villas you'll get at least twenty-five thousand roubles a year profit out of it.

GAEV. How utterly absurd!

LUBOV. I don't understand you at all, Ermolai Alexeyevitch.

LOPAKHIN. You will get twenty-five roubles a year for each dessiatin from the leaseholders at the very least, and if you advertise now I'm willing to bet that you won't have a vacant plot left by the autumn; they'll all go. In a word, you're saved. I congratulate you. Only, of course, you'll have to put things straight, and clean up.... For instance, you'll have to pull down all the old buildings, this house, which isn't any use to anybody now, and cut down the old cherry orchard....

LUBOV. Cut it down? My dear man, you must excuse me, but you don't understand anything at all. If there's anything interesting or remarkable in the whole province, it's this cherry orchard of ours.

LOPAKHIN. The only remarkable thing about the orchard is that it's very large. It only bears fruit every other year, and even then you don't know what to do with them; nobody buys any.

GAEV. This orchard is mentioned in the 'Encyclopaedic Dictionary.'

LOPAKHIN. [*Looks at his watch.*] If we can't think of anything and don't make up our minds to anything, then on August 22, both the cherry orchard and the whole estate will be up for auction. Make up your mind! I swear there's no other way out, I'll swear it again.

FIERS. In the old days, forty or fifty years back, they dried the cherries, soaked them and pickled them, and made jam of them, and it used to happen that...

GAEV. Be quiet, Fiers.

FIERS. And then we'd send the dried cherries off in carts to Moscow and Kharkov. And money! And the dried cherries were soft, juicy, sweet, and nicely scented.... They knew the way....

LUBOV. What was the way?

FIERS. They've forgotten. Nobody remembers.

PISCHIN. [*To* LUBOV ANDREYEVNA:] What about Paris? Eh? Did you eat frogs?

LUBOV. I ate crocodiles.

PISCHIN. To think of that, now.

LOPAKHIN. Up to now in the villages there were only the gentry and the labourers, and now the people who live in villas have arrived. All towns now, even small ones, are surrounded by villas. And it's safe to say that in twenty years' time the villa resident will be all over the place. At present he sits on his balcony and drinks tea, but it may well come to pass that he'll begin to cultivate his patch of land, and then your cherry orchard will be happy, rich, splendid....

GAEV. [*angry*] What rot!

[*Enter* VARYA *and* YASHA.]

VARYA. There are two telegrams for you, little mother. [*Picks out a key and noisily unlocks an antique cupboard.*] Here they are.

LUBOV. They're from Paris.... [*Tears them up without reading them.*] I've done with Paris.

GAEV. And do you know, Luba, how old this case is? A week ago I took out the bottom drawer; I looked and saw figures burnt out in it. That case was made exactly a hundred years ago. What do you think of that? What? We could celebrate its jubilee. It hasn't a soul of its own, but still, say what you will, it's a fine bookcase.

PISCHIN. [*astonished*] A hundred years.... Think of that!

GAEV. Yes... it's a real thing. [*Handling it.*] My dear and honoured case! I congratulate you on your existence, which has already for more than a hundred years been directed towards the bright ideals of good and justice; your silent call to productive labour has not grown less in the hundred years [*weeping*] during which you have upheld virtue and faith in a better future to the generations of our race, educating us up to ideals of goodness and to the knowledge of a common consciousness. [*Pause.*]

LOPAKHIN. Yes....

LUBOV. You're just the same as ever, Leon.

GAEV. [*a little confused*] Off the white on the right, into the corner pocket. Red ball goes into the middle pocket!

LOPAKHIN. [*Looks at his watch.*] It's time I went.

YASHA. [*Giving* LUBOV ANDREYEVNA *her medicine.*] Will you take your pills now?

PISCHIN. You oughtn't to take medicines, dear madam; they do you neither harm nor good.... Give them here, dear madam. [*Takes the pills, turns them out into the palm of his hand, blows on them, puts them into his mouth, and drinks some kvass.*] There!

LUBOV. [*frightened*] You're off your head!

PISCHIN. I've taken all the pills.

LOPAKHIN. Gormandizer! [*All laugh.*]

FIERS. They were here in Easter week and ate half a pailful of cucumbers.... [*Mumbles.*]

LUBOV. What's he driving at?

VARYA. He's been mumbling away for three years. We're used to that.

YASHA. Senile decay.

[CHARLOTTA IVANOVNA *crosses the stage, dressed in white: she is very thin and tightly laced; has a lorgnette at her waist.*]

LOPAKHIN. Excuse me, Charlotta Ivanovna, I haven't said 'How do you do' to you yet. [*Tries to kiss her hand.*]

CHARLOTTA. [*Takes her hand away.*] If you let people kiss your hand, then they'll want your elbow, then your shoulder, and then...

LOPAKHIN. My luck's out to-day! [*All laugh.*] Show us a trick, Charlotta Ivanovna!

LUBOV ANDREYEVNA. Charlotta, do us a trick.

CHARLOTTA. It's not necessary. I want to go to bed. [*Exit.*]

LOPAKHIN. We shall see each other in three weeks. [*Kisses* LUBOV ANDREYEVNA's *hand.*] Now, good-bye. It's time to go. [*To* GAEV:] See you again. [*Kisses* PISCHIN.] *Au revoir.* [*Gives his hand to* VARYA, *then to* FIERS *and to* YASHA:] I don't want to go away. [*To* LUBOV ANDREYEVNA:] If you think about the villas and make up your mind, then just let me know, and I'll raise a loan of 50,000 roubles at once. Think about it seriously.

VARYA. [*angrily*] Do go, now!

LOPAKHIN. I'm going, I'm going.... [*Exit.*]

GAEV. Snob. Still, I beg pardon.... Varya's going to marry him, he's Varya's young man.

VARYA. Don't talk too much, uncle.

LUBOV. Why not, Varya? I should be very glad. He's a good man.

PISCHIN. To speak the honest truth... he's a worthy man.... And my Dashenka... also says that... she says lots of things. [*Snores, but wakes up again at once.*] But still, dear madam, if you could lend me... 240 roubles... to pay the interest on my mortgage to-morrow...

VARYA. [*frightened*] We haven't got it, we haven't got it!

LUBOV. It's quite true. I've nothing at all.

PISCHIN. I'll find it all right. [*Laughs.*] I never lose hope. I used to think, 'Everything's lost now. I'm a dead man,' when, lo and behold, a railway was built over my land... and they paid me for it. And something else will happen to-day or to-morrow. Dashenka may win 20,000 roubles... she's got a lottery ticket.

LUBOV. The coffee's all gone, we can go to bed.

FIERS. [*Brushing* GAEV's *trousers; in an insistent tone*:] You've put on the wrong trousers again. What am I to do with you?

VARYA. [*quietly*] Anya's asleep. [*Opens window quietly.*] The sun has risen already; it isn't cold. Look, little mother: what lovely trees! And the air! The starlings are singing!

GAEV. [*Opens the other window.*] The whole garden's white. You haven't forgotten, Luba? There's that long avenue going straight, straight, like a stretched strap; it shines on moonlight nights. Do you remember? You haven't forgotten?

LUBOV. [*Looks out into the garden.*] Oh, my childhood, days of my innocence! In this nursery I used to sleep; I used to look out from here into the orchard. Happiness used to wake with me every morning, and then it was just as it is now; nothing has changed. [*Laughs from joy.*] It's all, all white! Oh, my orchard! After the dark autumns and the cold winters, you're young again, full of happiness, the angels of heaven haven't left you.... If only I could take my heavy burden off my breast and shoulders, if I could forget my past!

GAEV. Yes, and they'll sell this orchard to pay off debts. How strange it seems!

LUBOV. Look, there's my dead mother going in the orchard... dressed in white! [*Laughs from joy.*] That's she.

GAEV. Where?

VARYA. God bless you, little mother.

LUBOV. There's nobody there; I thought I saw somebody. On the right, at the turning by the summer-house, a white little tree bent down, looking just like a woman. [*Enter TROFIMOV in a worn student uniform and spectacles.*] What a marvellous garden! White masses of flowers, the blue sky....

TROFIMOV. Lubov Andreyevna! [*She looks round at him.*] I only want to show myself, and I'll go away. [*Kisses her hand warmly.*] I was told to wait till the morning, but I didn't have the patience.

[LUBOV ANDREYEVNA *looks surprised.*]

VARYA. [*Crying.*] It's Peter Trofimov.

TROFIMOV. Peter Trofimov, once the tutor of your Grisha.... Have I changed so much?

[LUBOV ANDREYEVNA embraces him and cries softly.]

GAEV. [*confused*] That's enough, that's enough, Luba.

VARYA. [*Weeps.*] But I told you, Peter, to wait till to-morrow.

LUBOV. My Grisha... my boy... Grisha... my son.

VARYA. What are we to do, little mother? It's the will of God.

TROFIMOV. [*softly, through his tears*] It's all right, it's all right.

LUBOV. [*Still weeping.*] My boy's dead; he was drowned. Why? Why, my friend? [*softly*] Anya's asleep in there. I am speaking so loudly, making such a noise.... Well, Peter? What's made you look so bad? Why have you grown so old?

TROFIMOV. In the train an old woman called me a decayed gentleman.

LUBOV. You were quite a boy then, a nice little student, and now your hair is not at all thick and you wear spectacles. Are you really still a student? [*Goes to the door.*]

TROFIMOV. I suppose I shall always be a student.

LUBOV. [*Kisses her brother, then* VARYA.] Well, let's go to bed.... And you've grown older, Leonid.

PISCHIN. [*Follows her.*] Yes, we've got to go to bed.... Oh, my gout! I'll stay the night here. If only, Lubov Andreyevna, my dear, you could get me 240 roubles to-morrow morning—

GAEV. Still the same story.

PISCHIN. Two hundred and forty roubles... to pay the interest on the mortgage.

LUBOV. I haven't any money, dear man.

PISCHIN. I'll give it back... it's a small sum....

LUBOV. Well, then, Leonid will give it to you.... Let him have it, Leonid.

GAEV. By all means; hold out your hand.

LUBOV. Why not? He wants it; he'll give it back.

[LUBOV ANDREYEVNA, TROFIMOV, PISCHIN, *and* FIERS *go out.* GAEV, VARYA, *and* YASHA *remain.*]

GAEV. My sister hasn't lost the habit of throwing money about. [*To* YASHA:] Stand off, do; you smell of poultry.

YASHA. [*Grins.*] You are just the same as ever, Leonid Andreyevitch.

GAEV. Really? [*To* VARYA:] What's he saying?

VARYA. [*To* YASHA:] Your mother's come from the village; she's been sitting in the servants' room since yesterday, and wants to see you....

YASHA. Bless the woman!

VARYA. Shameless man.

YASHA. A lot of use there is in her coming. She might have come tomorrow just as well. [*Exit.*]

VARYA. Mother hasn't altered a scrap, she's just as she always was. She'd give away everything, if the idea only entered her head.

GAEV. Yes.... [*Pause.*] If there's any illness for which people offer many remedies, you may be sure that particular illness is incurable, I think. I work my brains to their hardest. I've several remedies, very many, and that really means I've none at all. It would be nice to inherit a fortune from somebody, it would be nice to marry our Anya to a rich man, it would be nice to go to Yaroslav and try my luck with my aunt the Countess. My aunt is very, very rich.

VARYA. [*Weeps.*] If only God helped us.

GAEV. Don't cry. My aunt's very rich, but she doesn't like us. My sister, in the first place, married an advocate, not a noble.... [ANYA *appears in the doorway.*] She not only married a man who was not a noble, but she behaved herself in a way which cannot be described as proper. She's nice and kind and charming, and I'm very fond of her, but say what you will in her favour and you still have to admit that she's wicked; you can feel it in her slightest movements.

VARYA. [*Whispers.*] Anya's in the doorway.

GAEV. Really? [*Pause.*] It's curious, something's got into my right eye... I can't see properly out of it. And on Thursday, when I was at the District Court...

[*Enter* ANYA.]

VARYA. Why aren't you in bed, Anya?

ANYA. Can't sleep. It's no good.

GAEV. My darling! [*Kisses* ANYA's *face and hands.*] My child.... [*Crying.*] You're not my niece, you're my angel, you're my all.... Believe in me, believe...

ANYA. I do believe in you, uncle. Everybody loves you and respects you... but, uncle dear, you ought to say nothing, no more than that. What were you saying just now about my mother, your own sister? Why did you say those things?

GAEV. Yes, yes. [*Covers his face with her hand.*] Yes, really, it was awful. Save me, my God! And only just now I made a speech before a bookcase... it's so silly! And only when I'd finished I knew how silly it was.

VARYA. Yes, uncle dear, you really ought to say less. Keep quiet, that's all.

ANYA. You'd be so much happier in yourself if you only kept quiet.

GAEV. All right, I'll be quiet. [*Kisses their hands.*] I'll be quiet. But let's talk business. On Thursday I was in the District Court, and a lot of us met there together, and we began to talk of this, that, and the other, and now I think I can arrange a loan to pay the interest into the bank.

VARYA. If only God would help us!

GAEV. I'll go on Tuesday. I'll talk with them about it again. [*To* VARYA:] Don't howl. [*To* ANYA:] Your mother will have a talk to Lopakhin; he, of course, won't refuse... And when you've rested you'll go to Yaroslav to the Countess, your grandmother. So you see, we'll have three irons in the fire, and we'll be safe. We'll pay up the interest. I'm certain. [*Puts some sugar-candy into his mouth.*] I swear on my honour, on anything you will, that the estate will not be sold! [*excitedly*] I swear on my happiness! Here's my hand. You may call me a dishonourable wretch if I let it go to auction! I swear by all I am!

ANYA. [*She is calm again and happy.*] How good and clever you are, uncle. [*Embraces him.*] I'm happy now! I'm happy! All's well!

[*Enter* FIERS.]

FIERS. [*reproachfully*] Leonid Andreyevitch, don't you fear God? When are you going to bed?

GAEV. Soon, soon. You go away, Fiers. I'll undress myself. Well, children, bye-bye...! I'll give you the details to-morrow, but let's go to bed now. [*Kisses* ANYA *and* VARYA.] I'm a man of the eighties.... People don't praise those years much, but I can still say that I've suffered for my beliefs. The peasants don't love me for nothing, I assure you. We've got to learn to know the peasants! We ought to learn how....

ANYA. You're doing it again, uncle!

VARYA. Be quiet, uncle!

FIERS. [*angrily*] Leonid Andreyevitch!

GAEV. I'm coming, I'm coming.... Go to bed now. Off two cushions into the middle! I turn over a new leaf.... [*Exit. FIERS goes out after him.*]

ANYA. I'm quieter now. I don't want to go to Yaroslav, I don't like grandmother; but I'm calm now; thanks to uncle. [*Sits down.*]

VARYA. It's time to go to sleep. I'll go. There's been an unpleasantness here while you were away. In the old servants' part of the house, as you know, only the old people live—little old Efim and Polya and Evstigney, and Karp as well. They started letting some tramps or other spend the night there—I said nothing. Then I heard that they were saying that I had ordered them to be fed on peas and nothing else; from meanness, you see.... And it was all Evstigney's doing.... Very well, I thought, if that's what the matter is, just you wait. So I call Evstigney.... [*Yawns.*] He comes. 'What's this,' I say, 'Evstigney, you old fool.'... [*Looks at ANYA.*] Anya dear! [Pause.] She's dropped off.... [*Takes ANYA's arm.*] Let's go to bye-bye.... Come along!... [*Leads her.*] My darling's gone to sleep! Come on.... [*They go. In the distance, the other side of the orchard, a shepherd plays his pipe. TROFIMOV crosses the stage and stops on seeing VARYA and ANYA.*] Sh! She's asleep, asleep. Come on, dear.

ANYA. [*quietly, half-asleep*] I'm so tired... all the bells... uncle, dear! Mother and uncle!

VARYA. Come on, dear, come on! [*They go into* ANYA'S *room.*]

TROFIMOV. [*moved*] My sun! My spring!

Curtain.

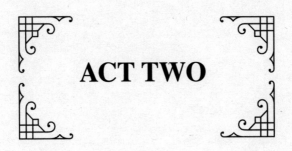

ACT TWO

[*In a field. An old, crooked shrine, which has been long abandoned; near it a well and large stones, which apparently are old tombstones, and an old garden seat. The road is seen to* GAEV'S *estate. On one side rise dark poplars, behind them begins the cherry orchard. In the distance is a row of telegraph poles, and far, far away on the horizon are the indistinct signs of a large town, which can only be seen on the finest and clearest days. It is close on sunset.* CHARLOTTA, YASHA, *and* DUNYASHA *are sitting on the seat;* EPIKHODOV *stands by and plays on a guitar; all seem thoughtful.* CHARLOTTA *wears a man's old peaked cap; she has unslung a rifle from her shoulders and is putting to rights the buckle on the strap.*]

CHARLOTTA. [*thoughtfully*] I haven't a real passport. I don't know how old I am, and I think I'm young. When I was a little girl my father and mother used to go round fairs and give very good performances and I used to do the *salto mortale* and various little things. And when papa and mamma died a German lady took me to her and began to teach me. I liked it. I grew up and became a governess. And where I came from and who I am, I don't know.... Who my parents were—perhaps they weren't married—I don't know. [*Takes a cucumber out of her pocket and eats.*] I don't know anything. [*Pause.*] I do want to talk, but I haven't anybody to talk to... I haven't anybody at all.

EPIKHODOV. [*Plays on the guitar and sings:*]

> 'What is this noisy earth to me,
> What matter friends and foes?'

I do like playing on the mandolin!

49

DUNYASHA. That's a guitar, not a mandolin. [*Looks at herself in a little mirror and powders herself.*]

EPIKHODOV. For the enamoured madman, this is a mandolin. [*Sings:*]

> 'Oh that the heart was warmed,
> By all the flames of love returned!'

[YASHA *sings too.*]

CHARLOTTA. These people sing terribly.... Foo! Like jackals.

DUNYASHA. [*To* YASHA:] Still, it must be nice to live abroad.

YASHA. Yes, certainly. I cannot differ from you there. [*Yawns and lights a cigar.*]

EPIKHODOV. That is perfectly natural. Abroad everything is in full complexity.

YASHA. That goes without saying.

EPIKHODOV. I'm an educated man, I read various remarkable books, but I cannot understand the direction I myself want to go—whether to live or to shoot myself, as it were. So, in case, I always carry a revolver about with me. Here it is. [*Shows a revolver.*]

CHARLOTTA. I've done. Now I'll go. [*Slings the rifle.*] You, Epikhodov, are a very clever man and very terrible; women must be madly in love with you. Brrr! [*Going.*] These wise ones are all so stupid. I've nobody to talk to. I'm always alone, alone; I've nobody at all... and I don't know who I am or why I live. [*Exit slowly.*]

EPIKHODOV. As a matter of fact, independently of everything else, I must express my feeling, among other things, that fate has been as pitiless in her dealings with me as a storm is to a small ship. Suppose, let us grant, I am wrong; then why did I wake up this morning, to give an example, and behold an enormous spider on my chest, like that? [*Shows with both hands.*] And if I do drink some kvass, why is it that there is bound to be something of the most indelicate nature in it, such as a beetle? [*Pause.*] Have you read Buckle? [*Pause.*] I should like to trouble you, Avdotya Fedorovna, for two words.

DUNYASHA. Say on.

EPIKHODOV. I should prefer to be alone with you. [*Sighs.*]

DUNYASHA. [*shy*] Very well, only first bring me my little cloak.... It's by the cupboard. It's a little damp here.

EPIKHODOV. Very well... I'll bring it.... Now I know what to do with my revolver. [*Takes guitar and exits, strumming.*]

YASHA. Two-and-twenty troubles! A silly man, between you and me and the gatepost. [*Yawns.*]

DUNYASHA. I hope to goodness he won't shoot himself. [*Pause.*] I'm so nervous, I'm worried. I went into service when I was quite a little girl, and now I'm not used to common life, and my hands are white, white as a lady's. I'm so tender and so delicate now; respectable and afraid of everything.... I'm so frightened. And I don't know what will happen to my nerves if you deceive me, Yasha.

YASHA. [*Kisses her.*] Little cucumber! Of course, every girl must respect herself; there's nothing I dislike more than a badly behaved girl.

DUNYASHA. I'm awfully in love with you; you're educated, you can talk about everything. [*Pause.*]

YASHA. [*Yawns.*] Yes. I think this: if a girl loves anybody, then that means she's immoral. [*Pause.*] It's nice to smoke a cigar out in the open air.... [*Listens.*] Somebody's coming. It's the mistress, and people with her. [DUNYASHA *embraces him suddenly.*] Go to the house, as if you'd been bathing in the river; go by this path, or they'll meet you and will think I've been meeting you. I can't stand that sort of thing.

DUNYASHA. [*Coughs quietly.*] My head's aching because of your cigar.

[*Exit.* YASHA *remains, sitting by the shrine. Enter* LUBOV ANDREYEVNA, GAEV, *and* LOPAKHIN.]

LOPAKHIN. You must make up your mind definitely—there's no time to waste. The question is perfectly plain. Are you willing to let the land for villas or no? Just one word, yes or no? Just one word!

LUBOV. Who's smoking horrible cigars here? [*Sits.*]

GAEV. They built that railway; that's made this place very handy. [*Sits.*] Went to town and had lunch... red in the middle! I'd like to go in now and have just one game.

LUBOV. You'll have time.

LOPAKHIN. Just one word! [*imploringly*] Give me an answer!

GAEV. [*Yawns.*] Really!

LUBOV. [*Looks in her purse.*] I had a lot of money yesterday, but there's very little to-day. My poor Varya feeds everybody on milk soup to save money, in the kitchen the old people only get peas, and I spend recklessly. [*Drops the purse, scattering gold coins.*] There, they are all over the place.

YASHA. Permit me to pick them up. [*Collects the coins.*]

LUBOV. Please do, Yasha. And why did I go and have lunch there?... A horrid restaurant with band and tablecloths smelling of soap.... Why do you drink so much, Leon? Why do you eat so much? Why do you talk so much? You talked again too much to-day in the restaurant, and it wasn't at all to the point—about the seventies and about decadents. And to whom? Talking to the waiters about decadents!

LOPAKHIN. Yes.

GAEV. [*Waves his hand.*] I can't be cured, that's obvious.... [*Irritably to* YASHA:] What's the matter? Why do you keep twisting about in front of me?

YASHA. [*Laughs.*] I can't listen to your voice without laughing.

GAEV. [*To his sister:*] Either he or I...

LUBOV. Go away, Yasha; get out of this....

YASHA. [*Gives purse to* LUBOV ANDREYEVNA.] I'll go at once. [*Hardly able to keep from laughing.*] This minute.... [*Exit.*]

LOPAKHIN. That rich man Deriganov is preparing to buy your estate. They say he'll come to the sale himself.

LUBOV. Where did you hear that?

LOPAKHIN. They say so in town.

GAEV. Our Yaroslav aunt has promised to send something, but I don't know when or how much.

LOPAKHIN. How much will she send? A hundred thousand roubles? Or two, perhaps?

LUBOV. I'd be glad of ten or fifteen thousand.

LOPAKHIN. You must excuse my saying so, but I've never met such frivolous people as you before, or anybody so unbusinesslike and peculiar. Here I am telling you in plain language that your estate will be sold, and you don't seem to understand.

LUBOV. What are we to do? Tell us, what?

LOPAKHIN. I tell you every day. I say the same thing every day. Both the cherry orchard and the land must be leased off for villas and at once, immediately—the auction is staring you in the face: Understand! Once you do definitely make up your minds to the villas, then you'll have as much money as you want and you'll be saved.

LUBOV. Villas and villa residents—it's so vulgar, excuse me.

GAEV. I entirely agree with you.

LOPAKHIN. I must cry or yell or faint. I can't stand it! You're too much for me! [*To* GAEV:] You old woman!

GAEV. Really!

LOPAKHIN. Old woman! [*Going out.*]

LUBOV. [*frightened*] No, don't go away, do stop; be a dear. Please. Perhaps we'll find some way out!

LOPAKHIN. What's the good of trying to think!

LUBOV. Please don't go away. It's nicer when you're here.... [*Pause.*] I keep on waiting for something to happen, as if the house is going to collapse over our heads.

GAEV. [*thinking deeply*] Double in the corner... across the middle....

LUBOV. We have been too sinful....

LOPAKHIN. What sins have you committed?

GAEV. [*Puts candy into his mouth.*] They say that I've eaten all my substance in sugar-candies. [*Laughs.*]

LUBOV. Oh, my sins.... I've always scattered money about without holding myself in, like a madwoman, and I married a man who made nothing but debts. My husband died of champagne—he drank terribly—and to my misfortune, I fell in love with another man and went off with him, and just at that time—it was my first punishment, a blow that hit me right on the head—here, in the river... my boy was drowned, and I went away, quite away, never to return, never to see this river again...I shut my eyes and ran without thinking, but he ran after me... without pity, without respect. I bought a villa near Mentone because he fell ill there, and for three years I knew no rest either by day or night; the sick man wore me out, and my soul dried up. And last year, when they had sold the villa to pay my debts, I went away to Paris, and there he robbed me of all I had and threw me over and went off with another woman. I tried to poison myself.... It was so silly, so shameful.... And suddenly I longed to be back in Russia, my own land, with my little girl.... [*Wipes her tears.*] Lord, Lord be merciful to me, forgive me my sins! Punish me no more! [*Takes a telegram out of her pocket.*] I had this to-day from Paris.... He begs my forgiveness, he implores me to return.... [*Tears it up.*] Don't I hear music? [*Listens.*]

GAEV. That is our celebrated Jewish band. You remember—four violins, a flute, and a double-bass.

LUBOV. So it still exists? It would be nice if they came along some evening.

LOPAKHIN. [*Listens.*] I can't hear.... [*Sings quietly.*] 'For money will the Germans make a Frenchman of a Russian.' [*Laughs.*] I saw such an awfully funny thing at the theatre last night.

LUBOV. I'm quite sure there wasn't anything at all funny. You oughtn't to go and see plays, you ought to go and look at yourself. What a grey life you lead, what a lot you talk unnecessarily.

LOPAKHIN. It's true. To speak the straight truth, we live a silly life. [*Pause.*] My father was a peasant, an idiot, he understood nothing, he didn't teach me, he was always drunk, and always used a stick on me. In point of fact, I'm a fool and an idiot too. I've never learned anything, my handwriting is bad, I write so that I'm quite ashamed before people, like a pig!

LUBOV. You ought to get married, my friend.

LOPAKHIN. Yes... that's true.

LUBOV. Why not to our Varya? She's a nice girl.

LOPAKHIN. Yes.

LUBOV. She's quite homely in her ways, works all day, and, what matters most, she's in love with you. And you've liked her for a long time.

LOPAKHIN. Well? I don't mind... she's a nice girl. [*Pause.*]

GAEV. I'm offered a place in a bank. Six thousand roubles a year.... Did you hear?

LUBOV. What's the matter with you! Stay where you are....

[*Enter* FIERS *with an overcoat.*]

FIERS. [*To* GAEV:] Please, sir, put this on, it's damp.

GAEV. [*Putting it on.*] You're a nuisance, old man.

FIERS. It's all very well.... You went away this morning without telling me. [*Examining* GAEV.]

LUBOV. How old you've grown, Fiers!

FIERS. I beg your pardon?

LOPAKHIN. She says you've grown very old!

FIERS. I've been alive a long time. They were already getting ready to marry me before your father was born.... [*Laughs.*] And when the Emancipation came I was already first valet. Only I didn't agree with the Emancipation and remained with my people.... [*Pause.*] I remember everybody was happy, but they didn't know why.

LOPAKHIN. It was very good for them in the old days. At any rate, they used to beat them.

FIERS. [*Not hearing.*] Rather. The peasants kept their distance from the masters and the masters kept their distance from the peasants, but now everything's all anyhow and you can't understand anything.

GAEV. Be quiet, Fiers. I've got to go to town tomorrow. I've been promised an introduction to a General who may lend me money on a bill.

LOPAKHIN. Nothing will come of it. And you won't pay your interest, don't you worry.

LUBOV. He's talking rubbish. There's no General at all.

[*Enter* TROFIMOV, ANYA, *and* VARYA.]

GAEV. Here they are.

ANYA. Mother's sitting down here.

LUBOV. [*tenderly*] Come, come, my dears.... [*Embracing* ANYA *and* VARYA.] If you two only knew how much I love you. Sit down next to me, like that. [*All sit down.*]

LOPAKHIN. Our eternal student is always with the ladies.

TROFIMOV. That's not your business.

LOPAKHIN. He'll soon be fifty, and he's still a student.

TROFIMOV. Leave off your silly jokes!

LOPAKHIN. Getting angry, eh, silly?

TROFIMOV. Shut up, can't you.

LOPAKHIN. [*Laughs.*] I wonder what you think of me?

TROFIMOV. I think, Ermolai Alexeyevitch, that you're a rich man, and you'll soon be a millionaire. Just as the wild beast which eats everything it finds is needed for changes to take place in matter, so you are needed too.

[*All laugh.*]

VARYA. Better tell us something about the planets, Peter.

LUBOV ANDREYEVNA. No, let's go on with yesterday's talk!

TROFIMOV. About what?

GAEV. About the proud man.

TROFIMOV. Yesterday we talked for a long time but we didn't come to anything in the end. There's something mystical about the proud man, in your sense. Perhaps you are right from your point of view, but if you take the matter simply, without complicating it, then what pride can there be, what sense can there be in it, if a man is imperfectly made, physiologically speaking, if in the vast majority of cases he is coarse and stupid and deeply unhappy? We must stop admiring one another. We must work, nothing more.

GAEV. You'll die, all the same.

TROFIMOV. Who knows? And what does it mean—you'll die? Perhaps a man has a hundred senses, and when he dies only the five known to us are destroyed and the remaining ninety-five are left alive.

LUBOV. How clever of you, Peter!

LOPAKHIN. [*ironically*] Oh, awfully!

TROFIMOV. The human race progresses, perfecting its powers. Everything that is unattainable now will some day be near at hand and comprehensible, but we must work, we must help with all our strength those who seek to know what fate will bring. Meanwhile in Russia only a very few of us work. The vast majority of those intellectuals whom I know seek for nothing, do nothing, and are at present incapable of hard work. They call themselves intellectuals, but they use 'thou' and 'thee' to their servants, they treat the peasants like animals, they learn badly, they read nothing seriously, they do absolutely nothing, about science they only talk, about art they understand little. They are all serious, they all have severe faces, they all talk about important things. They philosophize, and at the same time, the vast majority of us, ninety-nine out of a hundred, live like savages, fighting and cursing at the slightest opportunity, eating filthily, sleeping in the dirt, in stuffiness, with fleas, stinks, smells, moral filth, and so on... And it's obvious that all our nice talk is only carried on to distract ourselves and others. Tell me, where are those crèches we hear so much of? and where are those reading-rooms? People only write novels about them; they don't really exist. Only dirt, vulgarity, and Asiatic plagues really exist.... I'm afraid, and I don't at all like serious faces; I don't like serious conversations. Let's be quiet sooner.

LOPAKHIN. You know, I get up at five every morning, I work from morning till evening, I am always dealing with money—my own and other people's—and I see what people are like. You've only got to begin to do anything to find out how few honest, honourable people there are. Sometimes, when I can't sleep, I think: 'Oh Lord, you've given us huge forests, infinite fields, and endless horizons, and we, living here, ought really to be giants.'

LUBOV. You want giants, do you?... They're only good in stories, and even there they frighten one. [EPIKHODOV *enters at the back of the stage playing his guitar; thoughtfully:*] Epikhodov's there.

ANYA. [*thoughtfully*] Epikhodov's there.

GAEV. The sun's set, ladies and gentlemen.

TROFIMOV. Yes.

GAEV. [*not loudly, as if declaiming*] O Nature, thou art wonderful, thou shinest with eternal radiance! Oh, beautiful and indifferent one, thou whom we call mother, thou containest in thyself existence and death, thou livest and destroyest....

VARYA. [*entreatingly*] Uncle, dear!

ANYA. Uncle, you're doing it again!

TROFIMOV. You'd better double the red into the middle.

GAEV. I'll be quiet, I'll be quiet.

[*They all sit thoughtfully. It is quiet. Only the mumbling of* FIERS *is heard. Suddenly a distant sound is heard as if from the sky, the sound of a breaking string, which dies away sadly.*]

LUBOV. What's that?

LOPAKHIN. I don't know. It may be a bucket fallen down a well somewhere. But it's some way off.

GAEV. Or perhaps it's some bird... like a heron.

TROFIMOV. Or an owl.

LUBOV. [*Shudders.*] It's unpleasant, somehow. [*Pause.*]

FIERS. Before the misfortune the same thing happened. An owl screamed and the samovar hummed without stopping.

GAEV. Before what misfortune?

FIERS. Before the Emancipation. [*Pause.*]

LUBOV. You know, my friends, let's go in; it's evening now. [*To* ANYA:] You've tears in your eyes.... What is it, little girl? [*Embraces her.*]

ANYA. It's nothing, mother.

TROFIMOV. Some one's coming.

[*Enter a* TRAMP *in an old white peaked cap and overcoat. He is a little drunk.*]

TRAMP. Excuse me, may I go this way straight through to the station?

GAEV. You may. Go along this path.

TRAMP. I thank you from the bottom of my heart. [*Hiccups.*] Lovely weather.... [*Declaims:*] My brother, my suffering brother.... Come out on the Volga, you whose groans... [*To* VARYA:] Mademoiselle, please give a hungry Russian thirty copecks....

[VARYA *screams, frightened.*]

LOPAKHIN. [*angrily*] There's manners everybody's got to keep!

LUBOV. [*with a start*] Take this... here you are.... [*Feels in her purse.*] There's no silver.... It doesn't matter, here's gold.

TRAMP. I am deeply grateful to you! [*Exit. Laughter.*]

VARYA. [*frightened*] I'm going, I'm going.... Oh, little mother, at home there's nothing for the servants to eat, and you gave him gold.

LUBOV. What is to be done with such a fool as I am! At home I'll give you everything I've got. Ermolai Alexeyevitch, lend me some more!...

LOPAKHIN. Very well.

LUBOV. Let's go, it's time. And Varya, we've settled your affair; I congratulate you.

VARYA. [*Crying.*] You shouldn't joke about this, mother.

LOPAKHIN. Oh, feel me, get thee to a nunnery.

GAEV. My hands are all trembling; I haven't played billiards for a long time.

LOPAKHIN. Oh, feel me, nymph, remember me in thine orisons.

LUBOV. Come along; it'll soon be supper-time.

VARYA. He did frighten me. My heart is beating hard.

LOPAKHIN. Let me remind you, ladies and gentlemen, on August 22 the cherry orchard will be sold. Think of that!... Think of that!...

[*All go out except* TROFIMOV *and* ANYA.]

ANYA. [*Laughs.*] Thanks to the tramp who frightened Barbara, we're alone now.

TROFIMOV. Varya's afraid we may fall in love with each other and won't get away from us for days on end. Her narrow mind won't allow her to understand that we are above love. To escape all the petty and deceptive things which prevent our being happy and free, that is the aim and meaning of our lives. Forward! We go irresistibly on to that bright star which burns there, in the distance! Don't lag behind, friends!

ANYA. [*Clapping her hands.*] How beautifully you talk! [*Pause.*] It is glorious here to-day!

TROFIMOV. Yes, the weather is wonderful.

ANYA. What have you done to me, Peter? I don't love the cherry orchard as I used to. I loved it so tenderly, I thought there was no better place in the world than our orchard.

TROFIMOV. All Russia is our orchard. The land is great and beautiful, there are many marvellous places in it. [*Pause.*] Think, Anya, your grandfather, your great-grandfather, and all your ancestors were serf-owners, they owned living souls; and now, doesn't something human look at you from every cherry in the orchard, every leaf and every stalk? Don't you hear voices...? Oh, it's awful, your orchard is terrible; and when in the evening or at night you walk through the orchard, then the old bark on the trees sheds a dim light and the old cherry-trees seem to be dreaming of all that was a hundred, two hundred years ago, and are oppressed by their heavy visions. Still, at any rate, we've left those two hundred years behind us. So far we've gained nothing at all—we don't yet know what the past is to be to us—we only philosophize, we complain that we are dull, or we drink vodka. For it's so clear that in order to begin to live in the present we must first redeem the past, and that can only be done by suffering, by strenuous, uninterrupted labour. Understand that, Anya.

ANYA. The house in which we live has long ceased to be our house; I shall go away. I give you my word.

TROFIMOV. If you have the housekeeping keys, throw them down the well and go away. Be as free as the wind.

ANYA. [*enthusiastically*] How nicely you said that!

TROFIMOV. Believe me, Anya, believe me! I'm not thirty yet, I'm young, I'm still a student, but I have undergone a great deal! I'm as hungry as the winter, I'm ill, I'm shaken. I'm as poor as a beggar, and where haven't I been—fate has tossed me everywhere! But my soul is always my own; every minute of the day and the night it is filled with unspeakable presentiments. I know that happiness is coming, Anya, I see it already....

ANYA. [*thoughtful*] The moon is rising.

[EPIKHODOV *is heard playing the same sad song on his guitar. The moon rises. Somewhere by the poplars* VARYA *is looking for* ANYA *and calling,* 'Anya, where are you?']

TROFIMOV. Yes, the moon has risen. [*Pause.*] There is happiness, there it comes; it comes nearer and nearer; I hear its steps already. And if we do not see it we shall not know it, but what does that matter? Others will see it!

THE VOICE OF VARYA. Anya! Where are you?

TROFIMOV. That's Varya again! [*angry*] Disgraceful!

ANYA. Never mind. Let's go to the river. It's nice there.

TROFIMOV. Let's go. [*They go out.*]

THE VOICE OF VARYA. Anya! Anya!

Curtain.

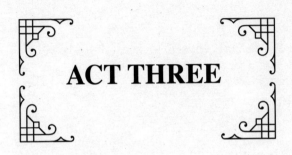

ACT THREE

[*A reception-room cut off from a drawing-room by an arch. Chandelier lighted. A Jewish band, the one mentioned in Act II, is heard playing in another room. Evening. In the drawing-room the* grand rond *is being danced. Voice of* SIMEONOV-PISCHIN 'Promenade a une paire!' *Dancers come into the reception-room; the first pair are* PISCHIN *and* CHARLOTTA IVANOVNA; *the second,* TROFIMOV *and* LUBOV ANDREYEVNA; *the third,* ANYA *and the* POST OFFICE CLERK; *the fourth,* VARYA *and the* STATION-MASTER, *and so on.* VARYA *is crying gently and wipes away her tears as she dances.* DUNYASHA *is in the last pair. They go off into the drawing-room,* PISCHIN *shouting,* 'Grand rond, balancez:' *and* 'Les cavaliers à genou et remerciez vos dames!' FIERS, *in a dress-coat, carries a tray with seltzer-water across. Enter* PISCHIN *and* TROFIMOV *from the drawing-room.*]

PISCHIN. I'm full-blooded and have already had two strokes; it's hard for me to dance, but, as they say, if you're in Rome, you must do as Rome does. I've got the strength of a horse. My dead father, who liked a joke, peace to his bones, used to say, talking of our ancestors, that the ancient stock of the Simeonov-Pischins was descended from that identical horse that Caligula made a senator.... [*Sits.*] But the trouble is, I've no money! A hungry dog only believes in meat. [*Snores and wakes up again immediately.*] So I... only believe in money....

TROFIMOV. Yes. There is something equine about your figure.

PISCHIN. Well... a horse is a fine animal... you can sell a horse.

[*Billiard playing can be heard in the next room.* VARYA *appears under the arch.*]

TROFIMOV. [*teasing*] Madame Lopakhin! Madame Lopakhin!

VARYA. [*angry*] Decayed gentleman!

TROFIMOV. Yes, I am a decayed gentleman, and I'm proud of it!

VARYA. [*bitterly*] We've hired the musicians, but how are they to be paid? [*Exit.*]

TROFIMOV. [*To* PISCHIN:] If the energy which you, in the course of your life, have spent in looking for money to pay interest had been used for something else, then, I believe, after all, you'd be able to turn everything upside down.

PISCHIN. Nietzsche... a philosopher... a very great, a most celebrated man... a man of enormous brain, says in his books that you can forge bank-notes.

TROFIMOV. And have you read Nietzsche?

PISCHIN. Well... Dashenka told me. Now I'm in such a position, I wouldn't mind forging them... I've got to pay 310 roubles the day after to-morrow... I've got 130 already.... [*Feels his pockets, nervously.*] I've lost the money! The money's gone! [*Crying.*] Where's the money? [*joyfully*] Here it is behind the lining... I even began to perspire.

[*Enter* LUBOV ANDREYEVNA *and* CHARLOTTA IVANOVNA.]

LUBOV. [*Humming a Caucasian dance.*] Why is Leonid away so long? What's he doing in town? [*To* DUNYASHA:] Dunyasha, give the musicians some tea.

TROFIMOV. Business is off, I suppose.

LUBOV. And the musicians needn't have come, and we needn't have got up this ball.... Well, never mind.... [*Sits and sings softly.*]

CHARLOTTA. [*Gives a pack of cards to* PISCHIN.] Here's a pack of cards, think of any one card you like.

PISCHIN. I've thought of one.

CHARLOTTA. Now shuffle. All right, now. Give them here, oh my dear Mr. Pischin. *Ein, zwei, drei!* Now look and you'll find it in your coat-tail pocket.

PISCHIN. [*Takes a card out of his coat-tail pocket.*] Eight of spades, quite right! [*surprised*] Think of that now!

CHARLOTTA. [*Holds the pack of cards on the palm of her hand. To* TROFIMOV:] Now tell me quickly. What's the top card?

TROFIMOV. Well, the queen of spades.

CHARLOTTA. Right! [*To* PISCHIN:] Well now? What card's on top?

PISCHIN. Ace of hearts.

CHARLOTTA. Right! [*Claps her hands, the pack of cards vanishes.*] How lovely the weather is to-day. [*A mysterious woman's voice answers her, as if from under the floor,* 'Oh yes, it's lovely weather, madam.'] You are so beautiful, you are my ideal. [*Voice,* 'You, madam, please me very much too.']

STATION-MASTER. [*Applauds.*] Madame ventriloquist, bravo!

PISCHIN. [*surprised*] Think of that, now! Delightful, Charlotte Ivanovna... I'm simply in love....

CHARLOTTA. In love? [*Shrugging her shoulders.*] Can you love? *Guter Mensch aber schlechter Musikant.*

TROFIMOV. [*Slaps* PISCHIN *on the shoulder.*] Oh, you horse!

CHARLOTTA. Attention please, here's another trick. [*Takes a shawl from a chair.*] Here's a very nice plaid shawl, I'm going to sell it.... [*Shakes it.*] Won't anybody buy it?

PISCHIN. [*astonished*] Think of that now!

CHARLOTTA. *Ein, zwei, drei.*

[*She quickly lifts up the shawl, which is hanging down.* ANYA *is standing behind it; she bows and runs to her mother, hugs her and runs back to the drawing-room amid general applause.*]

LUBOV. [*Applauds.*] Bravo, bravo!

CHARLOTTA. Once again! *Ein, zwei, drei!*

[*Lifts the shawl.* VARYA *stands behind it and bows.*]

PISCHIN. [*astonished*] Think of that, now.

CHARLOTTA. The end!

[*Throws the shawl at* PISCHIN, *curtseys and runs into the drawing-room.*]

PISCHIN. [*Runs after her.*] Little wretch.... What? Would you? [*Exit.*]

LUBOV. Leonid hasn't come yet. I don't understand what he's doing so long in town! Everything must be over by now. The estate must be sold; or, if the sale never came off, then why does he stay so long?

VARYA. [*Tries to soothe her.*] Uncle has bought it. I'm certain of it.

TROFIMOV. [*sarcastically*] Oh, yes!

VARYA. Grandmother sent him her authority for him to buy it in her name and transfer the debt to her. She's doing it for Anya. And I'm certain that God will help us and uncle will buy it.

LUBOV. Grandmother sent fifteen thousand roubles from Yaroslav to buy the property in her name—she won't trust us—and that wasn't even enough to pay the interest. [*Covers her face with her hands.*] My fate will be settled to-day, my fate....

TROFIMOV. [*Teasing* VARYA.] Madame Lopakhin!

VARYA. [*angry*] Eternal student! He's already been expelled twice from the university.

LUBOV. Why are you getting angry, Varya? He's teasing you about Lopakhin, well what of it? You can marry Lopakhin if you want to, he's a good, interesting man.... You needn't if you don't want to; nobody wants to force you against your will, my darling.

VARYA. I do look at the matter seriously, little mother, to be quite frank. He's a good man, and I like him.

LUBOV. Then marry him. I don't understand what you're waiting for.

VARYA. I can't propose to him myself, little mother. People have been talking about him to me for two years now, but he either says nothing, or jokes about it. I understand. He's getting rich, he's busy, he can't bother about me. If I had some money, even a little, even only a hundred roubles, I'd throw up everything and go away. I'd go into a convent.

TROFIMOV. How nice!

VARYA. [*To* TROFIMOV:] A student ought to have sense! [*gently, in tears*] How ugly you are now, Peter, how old you've grown! [*To* LUBOV ANDREYEVNA, *no longer crying:*] But I can't go on without working, little mother. I want to be doing something every minute.

[*Enter* YASHA.]

YASHA. [*Nearly laughing.*] Epikhodov's broken a billiard cue! [*Exit.*]

VARYA. Why is Epikhodov here? Who said he could play billiards? I don't understand these people. [*Exit.*]

LUBOV. Don't tease her, Peter, you see that she's quite unhappy without that.

TROFIMOV. She takes too much on herself, she keeps on interfering in other people's business. The whole summer she's given no peace to me or to Anya, she's afraid we'll have a romance all to ourselves. What has it to do with her? As if I'd ever given her grounds to believe I'd stoop to such vulgarity! We are above love.

LUBOV. Then I suppose I must be beneath love. [*in agitation*] Why isn't Leonid here? If I only knew whether the estate is sold or not! The disaster seems to me so improbable that I don't know what to think, I'm all at sea... I may scream... or do something silly. Save me, Peter. Say something, say something.

TROFIMOV. Isn't it all the same whether the estate is sold to-day or isn't? It's been all up with it for a long time; there's no turning back, the path's grown over. Be calm, dear, you shouldn't deceive yourself; for once in your life at any rate you must look the truth straight in the face.

LUBOV. What truth? You see where truth is, and where untruth is, but I seem to have lost my sight and see nothing. You boldly settle all important questions, but tell me, dear, isn't it because you're young, because you haven't had time to suffer till you settled a single one of your questions? You boldly look forward, isn't it because you cannot foresee or expect anything terrible, because so far life has been hidden from your young eyes? You are bolder, more honest, deeper than we are, but think only, be just a little magnanimous, and have mercy on me. I was born here, my father and mother lived here, my grandfather too, I love this house. I couldn't understand my life without that cherry orchard, and if it really must be sold, sell me with it! [*Embraces* TROFIMOV, *kisses his forehead.*] My son was drowned here.... [*Weeps.*] Have pity on me, good, kind man.

TROFIMOV. You know I sympathize with all my soul.

LUBOV. Yes, but it ought to be said differently, differently.... [*Takes another handkerchief, a telegram falls on the floor.*] I'm so sick at heart to-day, you can't imagine. Here it's so noisy, my soul shakes at every sound. I shake all over, and I can't go away by myself, I'm afraid of the silence. Don't judge me harshly, Peter... I love you, as if you belonged to my family. I'd gladly let Anya marry you, I swear it, only dear, you ought to work, finish your studies. You don't do anything, only fate throws you about from place to place, it's so odd.... Isn't it true? Yes? And you ought to do something to your beard to make it grow better [*Laughs.*] You are funny!

TROFIMOV. [*Picking up telegram.*] I don't want to be a Beau Brummel.

LUBOV. This telegram's from Paris. I get one every day.

Yesterday and to-day. That wild man is ill again, he's bad again.... He begs for forgiveness, and implores me to come, and I really ought to go to Paris to be near him. You look severe, Peter, but what can I do, my dear, what can I do; he's ill, he's alone, unhappy, and who's to look after him, who's to keep him away from his errors, to give him his medicine punctually? And why should I conceal it and say nothing about it; I love him, that's plain, I love him, I love him.... That love is a stone round my neck; I'm going with it to the bottom, but I love that stone and can't live without it. [*Squeezes* TROFIMOV's *hand.*] Don't think badly of me, Peter, don't say anything to me, don't say...

TROFIMOV. [*Weeping.*] For God's sake forgive my speaking candidly, but that man has robbed you!

LUBOV. No, no, no, you oughtn't to say that! [*Stops her ears.*]

TROFIMOV. But he's a wretch, you alone don't know it! He's a petty thief, a nobody....

LUBOV. [*angry, but restrained*] You're twenty-six or twenty-seven, and still a schoolboy of the second class!

TROFIMOV. Why not!

LUBOV. You ought to be a man, at your age you ought to be able to understand those who love. And you ought to be in love yourself, you must fall in love! [*angry*] Yes, yes! You aren't pure, you're just a freak, a queer fellow, a funny growth...

TROFIMOV. [*in horror*] What is she saying!

LUBOV. 'I'm above love!' You're not above love, you're just what our Fiers calls a bungler. Not to have a mistress at your age!

TROFIMOV. [*in horror*] This is awful! What is she saying? [*Goes quickly up into the drawing-room, clutching his head.*] It's awful... I can't stand it, I'll go away. [*Exit, but returns at once.*] All is over between us! [*Exit.*]

LUBOV. [*Shouts after him.*] Peter, wait! Silly man, I was joking! Peter! [*Somebody is heard going out and falling downstairs noisily.* ANYA *and* VARYA *scream; laughter is heard immediately.*] What's that?

[ANYA *comes running in, laughing.*]

ANYA. Peter's fallen downstairs! [*Runs out again.*]

LUBOV. This Peter's a marvel.

[*The* STATION-MASTER *stands in the middle of the drawing-room and recites 'The Magdalen' by Tolstoy. He is listened to, but he has only delivered a few lines when a waltz is heard from the front room, and the recitation is stopped. Everybody dances.* TROFIMOV, ANYA, VARYA, *and* LUBOV ANDREYEVNA *come in from the front room.*]

LUBOV. Well, Peter... you pure soul... I beg your pardon... let's dance.

[*She dances with* PETER. ANYA *and* VARYA *dance.* FIERS *enters and stands his stick by a side door.* YASHA *has also come in and looks on at the dance.*]

YASHA. Well, grandfather?

FIERS. I'm not well. At our balls some time back, generals and barons and admirals used to dance, and now we send for post-office clerks and the Station-master, and even they come as a favour. I'm very weak. The dead master, the grandfather, used to give everybody sealing-wax when anything was wrong. I've taken sealing-wax every day for twenty years, and more; perhaps that's why I still live.

YASHA. I'm tired of you, grandfather. [*Yawns.*] If you'd only hurry up and kick the bucket.

FIERS. Oh you... bungler! [*Mutters.*]

[TROFIMOV *and* LUBOV ANDREYEVNA *dance in the reception-room, then into the sitting-room.*]

LUBOV. *Merci.* I'll sit down. [*Sits.*] I'm tired.

[*Enter* ANYA.]

ANYA. [*excited*] Somebody in the kitchen was saying just now that the cherry orchard was sold to-day.

LUBOV. Sold to whom?

ANYA. He didn't say to whom. He's gone now. [*Dances out into the reception-room with* TROFIMOV.]

YASHA. Some old man was chattering about it a long time ago. A stranger!

FIERS. And Leonid Andreyevitch isn't here yet, he hasn't come. He's wearing a light, *demi-saison* overcoat. He'll catch cold. Oh these young fellows.

LUBOV. I'll die of this. Go and find out, Yasha, to whom it's sold.

YASHA. Oh, but he's been gone a long time, the old man. [*Laughs.*]

LUBOV. [*slightly vexed*] Why do you laugh? What are you glad about?

YASHA. Epikhodov's too funny. He's a silly man. Two-and-twenty troubles.

LUBOV. Fiers, if the estate is sold, where will you go?

FIERS. I'll go wherever you order me to go.

LUBOV. Why do you look like that? Are you ill? I think you ought to go to bed....

FIERS. Yes... [*With a smile.*] I'll go to bed, and who'll hand things round and give orders without me? I've the whole house on my shoulders.

YASHA. [*To* LUBOV ANDREYEVNA:] Lubov Andreyevna! I want to ask a favour of you, if you'll be so kind! If you go to Paris again, then please take me with you. It's absolutely impossible for me to stop here. [*Looking round; in an undertone:*] What's the good of talking about it, you see for yourself that this is an uneducated country, with an immoral population, and it's so dull. The food in the kitchen is beastly, and here's this Fiers walking about mumbling various inappropriate things. Take me with you, be so kind!

[*Enter* PISCHIN.]

PISCHIN. I come to ask for the pleasure of a little waltz, dear lady.... [LUBOV ANDREYEVNA *goes to him.*] But all the same, you wonderful woman, I must have 180 little roubles from you... I must.... [*They dance.*] 180 little roubles.... [*They go through into the drawing-room.*]

YASHA. [*Sings softly:*]

> 'Oh, will you understand
> My soul's deep restlessness?'

[*In the drawing-room a figure in a grey top-hat and in baggy check trousers is waving its hands and jumping about; there are cries of* 'Bravo, Charlotta Ivanovna!']

DUNYASHA. [*Stops to powder her face.*] The young mistress tells me to dance—there are a lot of gentlemen, but few ladies—and my head goes round when I dance, and my heart beats, Fiers Nicolaevitch; the Post Office clerk told me something just now which made me catch my breath. [*The music grows faint.*]

FIERS. What did he say to you?

DUNYASHA. He says, 'You're like a little flower.'

YASHA. [*Yawns.*] Impolite.... [*Exit.*]

DUNYASHA. Like a little flower. I'm such a delicate girl; I simply love words of tenderness.

FIERS. You'll lose your head.

[*Enter* EPIKHODOV.]

EPIKHODOV. You, Avdotya Fedorovna, want to see me no more than if I was some insect. [*Sighs.*] Oh, life!

DUNYASHA. What do you want?

EPIKHODOV. Undoubtedly, perhaps, you may be right. [*Sighs.*] But, certainly, if you regard the matter from the aspect, then you, if I may say so, and you must excuse my candidness, have absolutely reduced me to a state of mind. I know my fate, every day something unfortunate happens to me, and I've grown used to it a long time ago, I even look at my fate with a smile. You gave me your word, and though I...

DUNYASHA. Please, we'll talk later on, but leave me alone now. I'm meditating now. [*Plays with her fan.*]

EPIKHODOV. Every day something unfortunate happens to me, and I, if I may so express myself, only smile, and even laugh.

[VARYA *enters from the drawing-room.*]

VARYA. Haven't you gone yet, Simeon? You really have no respect for anybody. [*To* DUNYASHA:] You go away, Dunyasha. [*To* EPIKHODOV:] You play billiards and break a cue, and walk about the drawing-room as if you were a visitor!

EPIKHODOV. You cannot, if I may say so, call me to order.

VARYA. I'm not calling you to order, I'm only telling you. You just walk about from place to place and never do your work. Goodness only knows why we keep a clerk.

EPIKHODOV. [*offended*] Whether I work, or walk about, or eat, or play billiards, is only a matter to be settled by people of understanding and my elders.

VARYA. You dare to talk to me like that! [*furious*] You dare? You mean that I know nothing? Get out of here! This minute!

EPIKHODOV. [*nervous*] I must ask you to express yourself more delicately.

VARYA. [*beside herself*] Get out this minute. Get out! [*He goes to the door, she follows.*] Two-and-twenty troubles! I don't want any sign of you here! I don't want to see anything of you! [EPIKHODOV *has gone out; his voice can be heard outside:* 'I'll make a complaint against you.'] What, coming back? [*Snatches up the stick left by* FIERS *by the door.*] Go... go... go, I'll show you.... Are you going? Are you going? Well, then take that. [*She hits out as* LOPAKHIN *enters.*]

LOPAKHIN. Much obliged.

VARYA. [*angry but amused*] I'm sorry.

LOPAKHIN. Never mind. I thank you for my pleasant reception.

VARYA. It isn't worth any thanks. [*Walks away, then looks back and asks gently.*] I didn't hurt you, did I?

LOPAKHIN. No, not at all. There'll be an enormous bump, that's all.

VOICES FROM THE DRAWING-ROOM. Lopakhin's returned! Ermolai Alexeyevitch!

PISCHIN. Now we'll see what there is to see and hear what there is to hear... [*Kisses* LOPAKHIN.] You smell of cognac, my dear, my soul. And we're all having a good time.

[Enter LUBOV ANDREYEVNA.]

LUBOV. Is that you, Ermolai Alexeyevitch? Why were you so long? Where's Leonid?

LOPAKHIN. Leonid Andreyevitch came back with me, he's coming....

LUBOV. [*excited*] Well, what? Is it sold? Tell me?

LOPAKHIN. [*confused, afraid to show his pleasure*] The sale ended up at four o'clock.... We missed the train, and had to wait till half-past nine. [*Sighs heavily.*] Ooh! My head's going round a little.

[*Enter* GAEV; *in his right hand he carries things he has bought, with his left he wipes away his tears.*]

LUBOV. Leon, what's happened? Leon, well? [*impatiently, in tears*] Quick, for the love of God....

GAEV. [*Says nothing to her, only waves his hand; to* FIERS, *weeping:*] Here, take this.... Here are anchovies, herrings from Kertch.... I've had no food to-day.... I have had a time! [*The door from the billiard-room is open; the clicking of the balls is heard, and* YASHA'S *voice, 'Seven, eighteen!'* GAEV'S *expression changes, he cries no more.*] I'm awfully tired. Help me change my clothes, Fiers.

[*Goes out through the drawing-room;* FIERS *after him.*]

PISCHIN. What happened? Come on, tell us!

LUBOV. Is the cherry orchard sold?

LOPAKHIN. It is sold.

LUBOV. Who bought it?

LOPAKHIN. I bought it.

[LUBOV ANDREYEVNA *is overwhelmed; she would fall if she*

were not standing by an armchair and a table. VARYA takes
her keys off her belt, throws them on the floor, into the middle
of the room and goes out.]

LOPAKHIN. I bought it! Wait, ladies and gentlemen, please,
my head's going round, I can't talk.... [*Laughs.*] When we
got to the sale, Deriganov was there already. Leonid
Andreyevitch had only fifteen thousand roubles, and
Deriganov offered thirty thousand on top of the mortgage to
begin with. I saw how matters were, so I grabbed hold of
him and bid forty. He went up to forty-five, I offered fifty-
five. That means he went up by fives and I went up by tens....
Well, it came to an end. I bid ninety more than the mortgage;
and it stayed with me. The cherry orchard is mine now,
mine! [*Roars with laughter.*] My God, my God, the cherry
orchard's mine! Tell me I'm drunk, or mad, or dreaming....
[*Stamps his feet.*] Don't laugh at me! If my father and
grandfather rose from their graves and looked at the whole
affair, and saw how their Ermolai, their beaten and
uneducated Ermolai, who used to run barefoot in the winter,
how that very Ermolai has bought an estate, which is the
most beautiful thing in the world! I've bought the estate
where my grandfather and my father were slaves, where they
weren't even allowed into the kitchen. I'm asleep, it's only a
dream, an illusion.... It's the fruit of imagination, wrapped in
the fog of the unknown.... [*Picks up the keys, nicely smiling.*]
She threw down the keys, she wanted to show she was no
longer mistress here.... [*Jingles keys.*] Well, it's all one!
[*Hears the band tuning up.*] Eh, musicians, play, I want to
hear you! Come and look at Ermolai Lopakhin laying his axe
to the cherry orchard, come and look at the trees falling!

We'll build villas here, and our grandsons and great-grandsons will see a new life here.... Play on, music! [*The band plays.* LUBOV ANDREYEVNA *sinks into a chair and weeps bitterly.* LOPAKHIN *continues reproachfully:*] Why then, why didn't you take my advice? My poor, dear woman, you can't go back now. [*Weeps.*] Oh, if only the whole thing was done with, if only our uneven, unhappy life were changed!

PISCHIN. [*Takes his arm; in an undertone:*] She's crying. Let's go into the drawing-room and leave her by herself... come on.... [*Takes his arm and leads him out.*]

LOPAKHIN. What's that? Bandsmen, play nicely! Go on, do just as I want you to! [*ironically*] The new owner, the owner of the cherry orchard is coming! [*He accidentally knocks up against a little table and nearly upsets the candelabra.*] I can pay for everything! [*Exit with* PISCHIN.]

[*In the reception-room and the drawing-room nobody remains except* LUBOV ANDREYEVNA, *who sits huddled up and weeping bitterly. The band plays softly.* ANYA *and* TROFIMOV *come in quickly.* ANYA *goes up to her mother and goes on her knees in front of her.* TROFIMOV *stands at the drawing-room entrance.*]

ANYA. Mother! mother, are you crying? My dear, kind, good mother, my beautiful mother, I love you! Bless you! The cherry orchard is sold, we've got it no longer, it's true, true, but don't cry mother, you've still got your life before you, you've still your beautiful pure soul... Come with me, come, dear, away from here, come! We'll plant a new garden, finer than this, and you'll see it, and you'll understand, and deep joy, gentle joy will sink into your soul, like the evening sun, and you'll smile, mother! Come, dear, let's go!

Curtain.

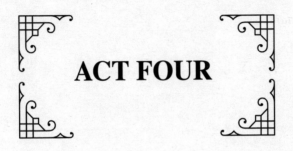

ACT FOUR

[*The stage is set as for Act I. There are no curtains on the windows, no pictures; only a few pieces of furniture are left; they are piled up in a corner as if for sale. The emptiness is felt. By the door that leads out of the house and at the back of the stage, portmanteaux and travelling paraphernalia are piled up. The door on the left is open; the voices of* VARYA *and* ANYA *can be heard through it.* LOPAKHIN *stands and waits.* YASHA *holds a tray with little tumblers of champagne. Outside,* EPIKHODOV *is tying up a box. Voices are heard behind the stage. The peasants have come to say good-bye. The voice of* GAEV *is heard:* 'Thank you, brothers, thank you.']

YASHA. The common people have come to say good-bye. I am of the opinion, Ermolai Alexeyevitch, that they're good people, but they don't understand very much.

[*The voices die away.* LUBOV ANDREYEVNA *and* GAEV *enter. She is not crying but is pale, and her face trembles; she can hardly speak.*]

GAEV. You gave them your purse, Luba. You can't go on like that, you can't!

LUBOV. I couldn't help myself, I couldn't! [*They go out.*]

LOPAKHIN. [*In the doorway, calling after them.*] Please, I ask you most humbly! Just a little glass to say good-bye. I didn't remember to bring any from town and I only found one bottle at the station. Please, do! [*Pause.*] Won't you really have any? [*Goes away from the door.*] If I only knew—I wouldn't have bought any. Well, I shan't drink any either.

[YASHA *carefully puts the tray on a chair.*] You have a drink, Yasha, at any rate.

YASHA. To those departing! And good luck to those who stay behind! [*Drinks.*] I can assure you that this isn't real champagne.

LOPAKHIN. Eight roubles a bottle. [*Pause.*] It's devilish cold here.

YASHA. There are no fires to-day, we're going away. [*Laughs.*]

LOPAKHIN. What's the matter with you?

YASHA. I'm just pleased.

LOPAKHIN. It's October outside, but it's as sunny and as quiet as if it were summer. Good for building. [*Looking at his watch and speaking through the door.*] Ladies and gentlemen, please remember that it's only forty-seven minutes till the train goes! You must go off to the station in twenty minutes. Hurry up.

[TROFIMOV, *in an overcoat, comes in from the grounds.*]

TROFIMOV. I think it's time we went. The carriages are waiting. Where the devil are my goloshes? They're lost. [*Through the door:*] Anya, I can't find my goloshes! I can't!

LOPAKHIN. I've got to go to Kharkov. I'm going in the same train as you. I'm going to spend the whole winter in

Kharkov. I've been hanging about with you people, going rusty without work. I can't live without working. I must have something to do with my hands; they hang about as if they weren't mine at all.

TROFIMOV. We'll go away now and then you'll start again on your useful labours.

LOPAKHIN. Have a glass.

TROFIMOV. I won't.

LOPAKHIN. So you're off to Moscow now?

TROFIMOV. Yes. I'll see them into town and to-morrow I'm off to Moscow.

LOPAKHIN. Yes.... I expect the professors don't lecture nowadays; they're waiting till you turn up!

TROFIMOV. That's not your business.

LOPAKHIN. How many years have you been going to the university?

TROFIMOV. Think of something fresh. This is old and flat. [*Looking for his goloshes.*] You know, we may not meet each other again, so just let me give you a word of advice on parting: 'Don't wave your hands about! Get rid of that habit of waving them about. And then, building villas and reckoning on their residents becoming freeholders in time—that's the same thing; it's all a matter of waving your hands about.... Whether I want to or not, you know, I like you. You've thin, delicate fingers, like those of an artist, and you've a thin, delicate soul....'

LOPAKHIN. [*Embraces him.*] Good-bye, dear fellow. Thanks for all you've said. If you want any, take some money from me for the journey.

TROFIMOV. Why should I? I don't want it.

LOPAKHIN. But you've nothing!

TROFIMOV. Yes, I have, thank you; I've got some for a translation. Here it is in my pocket. [*nervously*] But I can't find my goloshes!

VARYA. [*From the other room:*] Take your rubbish away! [*Throws a pair of rubber goloshes on to the stage.*]

TROFIMOV. Why are you angry, Varya? Hm! These aren't my goloshes!

LOPAKHIN. In the spring I sowed three thousand acres of poppies, and now I've made forty thousand roubles net profit. And when my poppies were in flower, what a picture it was! So I, as I was saying, made forty thousand roubles, and I mean I'd like to lend you some, because I can afford it. Why turn up your nose at it? I'm just a simple peasant....

TROFIMOV. Your father was a peasant, mine was a chemist, and that means absolutely nothing. [LOPAKHIN *takes out his pocket-book.*] No, no.... Even if you gave me twenty thousand I should refuse. I'm a free man. And everything that all you people, rich and poor, value so highly and so dearly hasn't the least influence over me; it's like a flock of down in the wind. I can do without you, I can pass you by. I'm strong and proud. Mankind goes on to the highest truths and to the highest happiness such as is only possible on earth, and I go in the front ranks!

LOPAKHIN. Will you get there?

TROFIMOV. I will. [*Pause.*] I'll get there and show others the way. [*Axes cutting the trees are heard in the distance.*]

LOPAKHIN. Well, good-bye, old man. It's time to go. Here we stand pulling one another's noses, but life goes its own way all the time. When I work for a long time, and I don't get tired, then I think more easily, and I think I get to understand why I exist. And there are so many people in Russia, brother, who live for nothing at all. Still, work goes on without that. Leonid Andreyevitch, they say, has accepted a post in a bank; he will get sixty thousand roubles a year.... But he won't stand it; he's very lazy.

ANYA. [*At the door.*] Mother asks if you will stop them cutting down the orchard until she has gone away.

TROFIMOV. Yes, really, you ought to have enough tact not to do that. [*Exit.*]

LOPAKHIN, All right, all right... yes, he's right. [*Exit.*]

ANYA. Has Fiers been sent to the hospital?

YASHA. I gave the order this morning. I suppose they've sent him.

ANYA. [*To* EPIKHODOV, *who crosses the room:*] Simeon Panteleyevitch, please make inquiries if Fiers has been sent to the hospital.

YASHA. [*offended*] I told Egor this morning. What's the use of asking ten times!

EPIKHODOV. The aged Fiers, in my conclusive opinion, isn't worth mending; his forefathers had better have him. I only envy him. [*Puts a trunk on a hat-box and squashes it.*] Well, of course. I thought so! [*Exit.*]

YASHA. [*grinning*] Two-and-twenty troubles.

VARYA. [*Behind the door.*] Has Fiers been taken away to the hospital?

ANYA. Yes.

VARYA. Why didn't they take the letter to the doctor?

ANYA. It'll have to be sent after him. [*Exit.*]

VARYA. [*In the next room.*] Where's Yasha? Tell him his mother's come and wants to say good-bye to him.

YASHA. [*Waving his hand.*] She'll make me lose all patience!

[DUNYASHA *has meanwhile been bustling round the luggage;
now that* YASHA *is left alone, she goes up to him.*]

DUNYASHA. If you only looked at me once, Yasha. You're
going away, leaving me behind.

[*Weeps and hugs him round the neck.*]

YASHA. What's the use of crying? [*Drinks champagne.*] In six
days I'll be again in Paris. To-morrow we get into the
express and off we go. I can hardly believe it. Vive la France!
It doesn't suit me here, I can't live here... it's no good. Well,
I've seen the uncivilized world; I have had enough of it.
[*Drinks champagne.*] What do you want to cry for? You
behave yourself properly, and then you won't cry.

DUNYASHA. [*Looks in a small mirror and powders her face.*]
Send me a letter from Paris. You know I loved you, Yasha, so
much! I'm a sensitive creature, Yasha.

YASHA. Somebody's coming.

[*He bustles around the luggage, singing softly. Enter* LUBOV
ANDREYEVNA, GAEV, ANYA, *and* CHARLOTTA IVANOVNA.]

GAEV. We'd better be off. There's no time left. [*Looks at*
YASHA.] Somebody smells of herring!

LUBOV. We needn't get into our carriages for ten minutes....
[*Looks round the room.*] Good-bye, dear house, old
grandfather. The winter will go, the spring will come, and
then you'll exist no more, you'll be pulled down. How much

these walls have seen! [*Passionately kisses her daughter.*]
My treasure, you're radiant, your eyes flash like two jewels!
Are you happy? Very?

ANYA. Very! A new life is beginning, mother!

GAEV. [*gaily*] Yes, really, everything's all right now. Before
the cherry orchard was sold we all were excited and we
suffered, and then, when the question was solved once and
for all, we all calmed down, and even became cheerful. I'm a
bank official now, and a financier... red in the middle; and
you, Luba, for some reason or other, look better, there's no
doubt about it.

LUBOV. Yes. My nerves are better, it's true. [*She puts on her
coat and hat.*] I sleep well. Take my luggage out, Yasha. It's
time. [*To* ANYA:] My little girl, we'll soon see each other
again.... I'm off to Paris. I'll live there on the money your
grandmother from Yaroslav sent along to buy the estate—
bless her!—though it won't last long.

ANYA. You'll come back soon, soon, mother, won't you? I'll
get ready, and pass the exam at the Higher School, and then
I'll work and help you. We'll read all sorts of books to one
another, won't we? [*Kisses her mother's hands.*] We'll read
in the autumn evenings; we'll read many books, and a
beautiful new world will open up before us.... [*thoughtfully*]
You'll come, mother....

LUBOV. I'll come, my darling. [*Embraces her.*]

[*Enter* LOPAKHIN. CHARLOTTA *is singing to herself.*]

GAEV. Charlotta is happy; she sings!

CHARLOTTA. [*Takes a bundle, looking like a wrapped-up baby.*] My little baby, bye-bye. [*The baby seems to answer,* 'Oua! Oua!'] Hush, my nice little boy. ['Oua! Oua!'] I'm so sorry for you! [*Throws the bundle back.*] So please find me a new place. I can't go on like this.

LOPAKHIN. We'll find one, Charlotta Ivanovna, don't you be afraid.

GAEV. Everybody's leaving us. Varya's going away... we've suddenly become unnecessary.

CHARLOTTA. I've nowhere to live in town. I must go away. [*Hums.*] Never mind.

[*Enter* PISCHIN.]

LOPAKHIN. Nature's marvel!

PISCHIN. [*puffing*] Oh, let me get my breath back.... I'm fagged out... My most honoured, give me some water....

GAEV. Come for money, what? I'm your humble servant, and I'm going out of the way of temptation. [*Exit.*]

PISCHIN. I haven't been here for ever so long... dear madam. [*To* LOPAKHIN:] You here? Glad to see you... man of immense brain... take this... take it.... [*Gives* LOPAKHIN *money.*] Four hundred roubles.... That leaves 840....

LOPAKHIN. [*Shrugs his shoulders in surprise.*] As if I were dreaming. Where did you get this from?

PISCHIN. Stop... it's hot.... A most unexpected thing happened. Some Englishmen came along and found some white clay on my land.... [*To* LUBOV ANDREYEVNA:] And here's four hundred for you... beautiful lady.... [*Gives her money.*] Give you the rest later.... [*Drinks water.*] Just now a young man in the train was saying that some great philosopher advises us all to jump off roofs. 'Jump!' he says, and that's all. [*astonished*] To think of that, now! More water!

LOPAKHIN. Who were these Englishmen?

PISCHIN. I've leased off the land with the clay to them for twenty-four years.... Now, excuse me, I've no time.... I must run off.... I must go to Znoikov and to Kardamonov... I owe them all money.... [*Drinks.*] Good-bye. I'll come in on Thursday.

LUBOV. We're just off to town, and to-morrow I go abroad.

PISCHIN. [*agitated*] What? Why to town? I see furniture... trunks.... Well, never mind. [*Crying.*] Never mind. These Englishmen are men of immense intellect.... Never mind.... Be happy.... God will help you.... Never mind.... Everything in this world comes to an end.... [*Kisses* LUBOV ANDREYEVNA'S *hand.*] And if you should happen to hear that my end has come, just remember this old... horse and say: 'There was one such and such a Simeonov-Pischin, God bless his soul....' Wonderful weather... yes.... [*Exit deeply*

moved, but returns at once and says in the door:] Dashenka
sent her love! [*Exit.*]

LUBOV. Now we can go. I've two anxieties, though. The first
is poor Fiers [*Looks at her watch.*] We've still five minutes....

ANYA. Mother, Fiers has already been sent to the hospital.
Yasha sent him off this morning.

LUBOV. The second is Varya. She's used to getting up early
and to work, and now she's no work to do she's like a fish
out of water. She's grown thin and pale, and she cries, poor
thing.... [*Pause.*] You know very well, Ermolai Alexeyevitch,
that I used to hope to marry her to you, and I suppose you
are going to marry somebody? [*Whispers to* ANYA, *who nods
to* CHARLOTTA, *and they both go out.*] She loves you, she's
your sort, and I don't understand, I really don't, why you
seem to be keeping away from each other. I don't
understand!

LOPAKHIN. To tell the truth, I don't understand it myself. It's
all so strange.... If there's still time, I'll be ready at once...
Let's get it over, once and for all; I don't feel as if I could
ever propose to her without you.

LUBOV. Excellent. It'll only take a minute. I'll call her.

LOPAKHIN. The champagne's very appropriate. [*Looking at
the tumblers.*] They're empty, somebody's already drunk
them. [YASHA coughs.] I call that licking it up....

LUBOV. [*animated*] Excellent. We'll go out. Yasha, *allez*. I'll call her in.... [*At the door.*] Varya, leave that and come here. Come! [*Exit with* YASHA.]

LOPAKHIN. [*Looks at his watch.*] Yes.... [*Pause.*]

[*There is a restrained laugh behind the door, a whisper, then* VARYA *comes in.*]

VARYA. [*Looking at the luggage in silence.*] I can't seem to find it....

LOPAKHIN. What are you looking for?

VARYA. I packed it myself and I don't remember. [*Pause.*]

LOPAKHIN. Where are you going to now, Barbara Mihailovna?

VARYA. I? To the Ragulins.... I've got an agreement to go and look after their house... as housekeeper or something.

LOPAKHIN. Is that at Yashnevo? It's about fifty miles. [*Pause.*] So life in this house is finished now....

VARYA. [*Looking at the luggage.*] Where is it?... perhaps I've put it away in the trunk.... Yes, there'll be no more life in this house....

LOPAKHIN. And I'm off to Kharkov at once... by this train. I've a lot of business on hand. I'm leaving Epikhodov here... I've taken him on.

VARYA. Well, well!

LOPAKHIN. Last year at this time the snow was already falling, if you remember, and now it's nice and sunny. Only it's rather cold.... There's three degrees of frost.

VARYA. I didn't look. [*Pause.*] And our thermometer's broken.... [*Pause.*]

VOICE AT THE DOOR. Ermolai Alexeyevitch!

LOPAKHIN. [*as if he has long been waiting to be called*] This minute. [*Exits quickly.*]

[VARYA, *sitting on the floor, puts her face on a bundle of clothes and weeps gently. The door opens.* LUBOV ANDREYEVNA *enters carefully.*]

LUBOV. Well? [*Pause.*] We must go.

VARYA. [*Not crying now, wipes her eyes.*] Yes, it's quite time, little mother. I'll get to the Ragulins to-day, if I don't miss the train....

LUBOV. [*At the door.*] Anya, put on your things. [*Enter* ANYA, *then* GAEV, CHARLOTTA IVANOVNA. GAEV *wears a warm overcoat with a cape. A servant and drivers come in.* EPIKHODOV *bustles around the luggage.*] Now we can go away.

ANYA. [*joyfully*] Away!

GAEV. My friends, my dear friends! Can I be silent, in leaving this house for evermore?—can I restrain myself, in saying farewell, from expressing those feelings which now fill my whole being...?

ANYA. [*imploringly*] Uncle!

VARYA. Uncle, you shouldn't!

GAEV. [*stupidly*] Double the red into the middle.... I'll be quiet.

[*Enter* TROFIMOV, *then* LOPAKHIN.]

TROFIMOV. Well, it's time to be off.

LOPAKHIN. Epikhodov, my coat!

LUBOV. I'll sit here one more minute. It's as if I'd never really noticed what the walls and ceilings of this house were like, and now I look at them greedily, with such tender love....

GAEV. I remember, when I was six years old, on Trinity Sunday, I sat at this window and looked and saw my father going to church....

LUBOV. Have all the things been taken away?

LOPAKHIN. Yes, all, I think. [*To* EPIKHODOV, *putting on his coat:*] You see that everything's quite straight, Epikhodov.

EPIKHODOV. [*hoarsely*] You may depend upon me, Ermolai Alexeyevitch!

LOPAKHIN. What's the matter with your voice?

EPIKHODOV. I swallowed something just now; I was having a drink of water.

YASHA. [*suspiciously*] What manners....

LUBOV. We go away, and not a soul remains behind.

LOPAKHIN. Till the spring.

VARYA. [*Drags an umbrella out of a bundle, and seems to be waving it about.* LOPAKHIN *appears to be frightened.*] What are you doing?... I never thought...

TROFIMOV. Come along, let's take our seats... it's time! The train will be in directly.

VARYA. Peter, here they are, your goloshes, by that trunk. [*in tears*] And how old and dirty they are....

TROFIMOV. [*Putting them on.*] Come on!

GAEV. [*deeply moved, nearly crying*] The train... the station.... Cross in the middle, a white double in the corner....

LUBOV. Let's go!

LOPAKHIN. Are you all here? There's nobody else? [*Locks the side-door on the left.*] There's a lot of things in there. I must lock them up. Come!

ANYA. Good-bye, home! Good-bye, old life!

TROFIMOV. Welcome, new life! [*Exit with* ANYA.]

[VARYA *looks round the room and goes out slowly.* YASHA *and* CHARLOTTA, *with her little dog, go out.*]

LOPAKHIN. Till the spring, then! Come on... till we meet again! [*Exit.*]

[LUBOV ANDREYEVNA *and* GAEV *are left alone. They might almost have been waiting for that. They fall into each other's arms and sob restrainedly and quietly, fearing that somebody might hear them.*]

GAEV. [*in despair*] My sister, my sister....

LUBOV. My dear, my gentle, beautiful orchard! My life, my youth, my happiness, good-bye! Good-bye!

ANYA'S VOICE. [*gaily*] Mother!

TROFIMOV'S VOICE. [*gaily, excited*] Coo-ee!

LUBOV. To look at the walls and the windows for the last time.... My dead mother used to like to walk about this room....

GAEV. My sister, my sister!

ANYA'S VOICE. Mother!

TROFIMOV'S VOICE. Coo-ee!

LUBOV. We're coming! [*They go out.*]

[*The stage is empty. The sound of keys being turned in the locks is heard, and then the noise of the carriages going away. It is quiet. Then the sound of an axe against the trees is heard in the silence sadly and by itself. Steps are heard.* FIERS *comes in from the door on the right. He is dressed as usual, in a short jacket and white waistcoat; slippers on his feet. He is ill. He goes to the door and tries the handle.*]

FIERS. It's locked. They've gone away. [*Sits on a sofa.*] They've forgotten about me.... Never mind, I'll sit here.... And Leonid Andreyevitch will have gone in a light overcoat instead of putting on his fur coat.... [*Sighs anxiously.*] I didn't see.... Oh, these young people! [*Mumbles something that cannot be understood.*] Life's gone on as if I'd never lived. [*Lying down.*] I'll lie down.... You've no strength left in you, nothing left at all.... Oh, you... bungler!

[*He lies without moving. The distant sound is heard, as if from the sky, of a breaking string, dying away sadly. Silence follows it, and only the sound is heard, some way away in the orchard, of the axe falling on the trees.*]

Curtain.